# WHISPERS
## in the
# VINEYARD

WE APPRECIATE
YOUR SERVICE!
W₂W Staff

# WHISPERS in the VINEYARD

*A Vineyard Keeper's Meditations*

SECOND EDITION

DEANNA L. MARTIN

TATE PUBLISHING
AND ENTERPRISES, LLC

Published by Tate Publishing & Enterprises, LLC
127 E. Trade Center Terrace | Mustang, Oklahoma 73064 USA
1.888.361.9473 | www.tatepublishing.com

Tate Publishing is committed to excellence in the publishing industry. The company reflects the philosophy established by the founders, based on Psalm 68:11,
*"The Lord gave the word and great was the company of those who published it."*

Book design copyright © 2013 by Tate Publishing, LLC. All rights reserved.
*Cover design by Rtor Maghuyop*
*Interior design by Gram Telen*

Published in the United States of America

ISBN: 978-1-62902-725-8
1. Religion / Christian Life / Personal Growth
2. Religion / Christian Life / Spiritual Growth
13.10.31

In loving memory of my first-born son,
Joshua Michael Kirkland,
whom the Heavenly Vineyard
Keeper took home to heaven
July 29, 1993.

# Dedications

### AND

# Acknowledgements

This book is dedicated to my dear husband, without whose patience, love and instruction I would have never become a Vineyard Keeper. I would have never known the riches and romance of the vineyard; nor would I have had the privilege of sharing in the Lord's revelations of grace to me as I labored in the field. Thank you for introducing me to the world of the Vineyard Keeper!

I also want to thank my parents, Earl and Ginny Schafer, for raising me to know and love the *Lord of the Harvest* and for teaching me to be sensitive to His voice.

Finally to my precious sons (Joshua, Caleb and Zachary): thank you for giving me numerous opportunities to learn that anything worth doing takes time, patience and love. Thank you for bringing so much joy into my life. I love you all.

# CONTENTS

# PREFACE

I have never been the outdoor, country girl type. Never did I dream of working with the fertile earth and getting my fingernails dirty. (*Heavens, I might break one!*) My hobbies have always been inside activities...reading, sewing, singing, tending to my many houseplants, and caring for my three boys (Joshua, Caleb and Zachary). I certainly never envisioned myself as a farmer. (*Who me? In overalls... driving a tractor? No Way!*)

But God... (*What wonderful comforting words these are!*) It is *He* that has our future in His hands, and His plans are the very *BEST!*

> "For I know the plans I have for you", declares the Lord, "plans to prosper you and not to harm you, plans to give you hope and a future".
>
> Jeremiah 29:11

Years ago, Bill and I began to dream of having our own grape vineyard. This dream became a reality and for about a decade we saw our vines produce tons of magnificent grapes. These vines, however, needed considerable care. I had no idea what toil lay before me and the parallels God would reveal to me; parallels between me training and caring for the vineyard and His training and caring for me. These similarities were so striking as to be unmistakable. The love of our *Vineyard Keeper* and His meticulous care for us; the rationale for some of the apparently painful processes He orchestrates, *and allows*, in our lives; these became clearer to me as I journeyed deeper into this new world.

After many seasons working in the vineyard, God still speaks to me through the vines. Oft times while working at the same thing I have done so mindlessly thousands of times before, I find myself suddenly face-to-face with another analogy of God's incredible care for us.

In the following pages, I have endeavored to put some of these precious truths on paper as God has revealed them to me in our walk through the vineyard. My hope is that you, too, will be blessed as you share in these revelations. So put your feet up, pour yourself a cup of your favorite beverage, enjoy the pictures in the center for illustration of each meditation, and join me as I share His...

Whispers in the Vineyard!

# The Dream

God had new challenges ahead for me that I could not have imagined. I married Bill, my wonderful, godly, horticulturally gifted man, and we began to seek God's direction for us as a family. Our Heavenly Father faithfully answered and gave us a dream! We would have a vineyard! God had given Bill both the ability and the "know-how"; both of us had the desire (*something brand new for me*) and now we had the opportunity. I didn't know all that would be involved in accomplishing this dream, but we had a dream! (*Have you ever noticed...dreams are kinda fuzzy around the edges...lacking some critical facts of reality?*)

We already had the field...12 acres of the most fertile river-bottom land in Texas and a well of endlessly available water. We considered the cost and labor to start. I listened to *talk* of the ***incredible*** amount of work that would be involved, but I didn't really *HEAR*. I was nowhere near being prepared for the backbreaking work and extremely complicated course that lie ahead.

You know...we think we want to know the future and what lies ahead. However, if we were shown the hardships ahead of us, most likely we would dig in our heels and try to get out of it. In retrospect, that is how I see the vineyard project. If I had really had *any* clue as to what lie ahead and the labor intensive, and oft-times discouraging, process we were about to embark upon, I doubt I would have had the courage to go ahead with it. **But what reward there is in completing a difficult course and coming through to the end of it!**

We considered and planned as best we could with the knowledge we had. Much like the man in the story Jesus told (when speaking to one of the many crowds that hung on His every word), we counted the cost of the project before we began. His advice is recorded in the book of Luke.

> Suppose one of you wants to build a tower. Will he not first sit down and estimate the cost to see if he has enough money to complete it? For if he lays the foundation and is not able to finish it, everyone who sees it will ridicule him saying, 'This fellow began to build and was not able to finish'.

> Luke 14:28-30

We sought counsel from the Lord, as well as from godly men.

> "Plans fail for lack of counsel, but with many advisers they succeed."

> Proverbs 15:22

And thus we forged ahead. **"Operation–Martin Vineyard"** was launched!

Prepare the ground by leveling it & destroy existing weeds and vegetation

Pound 50 Rows of 110 stakes each (that's 5500 stakes!) into the dry (I mean *really* dry) Texas earth!

Run 3 levels of wire the length of each row...(That is 100 lengths of wire, approx. 900' each time!)

Clip each of the 3 wires to every stake...that's 16,500 clips!

Dig underground trench for PVC pipes that will become the all important irrigation system.

Install 100 upright PVC lines to connect to the underground pipes on the center end of each row.

Run drip line hose on each of the fifty 900' rows.

Connect drip line to each of the 100 upright PVC lines.

Clip the drip line to the bottom row of wire on each of the 50 rows.

Install a 'one gallon-per-hour' drip emitter at each stake...that's 5500 emitters!

Dig 5500 holes for plants with a post-hole digger. *(Unbelievably tough job, this one!)*

Plant a baby grapevine at each stake...that's 5500 grapevines.

Begin watering the vines and watch them grow... and grow!

After all this was completed... We **HAD A VINEYARD!!**

MEDITATION TWO
# CHANGING SEASONS

As individuals living in the sea of humanity, we all experience changing seasons in our lives; times of joy and times of sadness. Our changing seasons mirror the four seasons of the earth...winter, spring, summer and autumn. Each season brings different tasks, joys and challenges and each season passes, in its turn.

When Winter enters our lives, He brings dark, cold, despairing days when we must struggle to stay close to the Fire (our Lord) and try to remember that spring *will come* again. Then Spring blows in with her bright and balmy days, filled with laughter and joy, and the promise of good things to come.

The long, scorching days of Summer follow, filled with hot drudgery trying to satisfy a demanding taskmaster. We yearn to be out of the heat and our parched souls long for cool, thirst quenching relief. In the midst of the heat, we look forward to the cooler, lazier days of autumn.

When at last Autumn's refreshing chill is felt on the breeze, she ushers in new and lovely colors in our lives. We can begin to rest and be refreshed; review the lessons learned in the heat and prepare for the future.

The Author of Ecclesiastes recognized these different life cycles and that they are common to all of mankind.

> "There is a time for everything, and a season for every activity under heaven:
> A time to be born and a time to die, A time to plant and a time to uproot,
> A time to kill and a time to heal, A time to tear down and a time to build,
> A time to weep and a time to laugh, A time to mourn and a time to dance
> A time to tear and a time to mend, A time to be silent and a time to speak,
> A time to love and a time to hate, A time for war and a time for peace."

Ecclesiastes 3:1-4, 7

Whatever the changing winds of life blow our way, we must cling to the **Lord of our Seasons**, for He has ordained these times of our hearts and knows how to lead us through them with peace and victory!

# Four Seasons in The Vineyard

## Winter

Cold, hard winters are one of the greatest allies in a vineyard keeper's ongoing battle against insects and diseases. While I am curled up in front of a crackling fire with my hot chocolate and a good book, Winter is doing his work. The sub-freezing temperatures lessen insects like grasshoppers, crickets and others that feed on the grapevine's tender foliage. There is also at least one deadly disease that can completely destroy the vineyard unless a very cold winter intervenes and freezes it dead!

Winter serves another valuable purpose in our vineyard. Even as we need to put up our feet and relax after the frantic activity of a growing season, so our vines need a period of rest. No new growth, no fruit to support, just lazy dormancy to prepare and store up energy for a new season of vigorous growth.

This is also a time when they deepen their roots further so they can support greater fruit the following year.

Then comes..?

# Spring

A time of refreshing, balmy warmth;
Fresh vibrant colors
After monochrome, drab browns;
Beehive-busy after lazy winter pursuits.

I have *so much* to do now! Thankfully the daylight hours are lengthening. The work seems limitless as we prepare the vineyard for the new season. Burgeoning buds are threatening to burst forth with their new growth and there is an infinite amount of pruning to be done. Tying the vigorous new vine growth to the wires is an absolutely overwhelming task!

It is a time of exciting possibilities...
*(We could have a bumper crop this year!)*
And rewarding weariness...
*(I can't believe I've pruned and tied 300 vines today!*
*Only 5200 plants to go!!!)*
Endless pruning and tying of new growth...
*(I am amazed at the rapid growth in the spring!)*
Fertilizing each and every plant for healthy growth!
*(This has to be done by hand...very time consuming.)*
Constant monitoring of the drip system...
*(We must make sure all plants are getting water)*
Spraying for insects, weeds and diseases;
and mowing and mowing and more mowing.

This blends into..?

# SUMMER

There is the continuous training and tying of vines:
New fruit must be kept insect and disease free.
We must water frequently, and add more fertilizer,
Oops! Watch out for those water-leaching weeds...
They've gotta go!
Watching, working, waiting and *PRAYING*!!!
Anticipation upon seeing the fruit ripen
And turn translucent...They are almost ripe!
Excitement! Hope!
Test the fruit often until just the right brix
(sugar) level is reached.
(*Did you know that grapes have the highest sugar
content of any fruit in the world?*)

## FINALLY IT'S HERE! HARVEST TIME!

We gather laborers, picking buckets, pruning shears, and lots of cold drinks for the laborers who must toil in the smothering Texas heat and humidity! It takes long days to pick the four varieties of grapes we grow, and each variety ripens at a different time.

It is such beautifully, elegant fruit! All the exhausting work has paid off. We are so thankful and proud and we do not forget to thank the *Lord* of our harvest!

When finally, with a sigh of relief, we coast into..?

# AUTUMN

Shortening daylight hours
Marvelous cooling of days and nights begins
Watering the vines less often to help them prepare
for dormancy
Resting from the tedious day-to-day work of the past
nine months.

The slower pace of this season gives us time to make repairs that have been delayed because of the "tyranny of the urgent"; i.e. repairs on equipment, end posts, wires, the irrigation system, etc.

With a sigh of relief, we slow down and take time to appraise the past year's accomplishments and disappointments. During this time of reflection, we assess any new procedures we have used during this season. Were they good or bad? Did they increase our quality and/or quantity of fruit?

Through this process of evaluation we determine which practices we want to keep and which we will change in the future. Since each growing season is different, each presents its own set of challenges, rewards and pains. Evaluation of each facet of the vineyard is a necessary step to insure the quality and longevity of the vines and their continued quality fruit production.

Before we know it, another season begins. Another...

# SEASON IN THE VINEYARD!

# VINEYARD KEEPER

I must confess I had no idea what a HUGE job caring for 12 acres of grapes would be! There are so many things to think of and consider in caring for and protecting the grapevines.

Truth is, being a Vineyard Keeper is a tough job, and not for the faint hearted. Through the years, I have discovered there are specific qualities you need if you want to be successful at it.

A Vineyard Keeper needs to care so deeply for the welfare of his vines that he is willing to do *whatever is necessary* for their <u>long-term</u> health.

> "I am the true vine, and my Father is the gardener. *(Vineyard Keeper)* He cuts off every branch in me that bears no fruit, while every branch that does bear fruit he prunes so that it will be even more fruitful."
>
> John 15:1-2

Though I fell in love with the grapevines that very first season, I found they are very like children that need constant training. They require daily tending and monitoring of their health. I often found myself talking to them, explaining why I was removing a beautiful "bull shoot", shortening a cordon, or removing some of their fruit.

However, my *entire reason* for being in the vineyard was to get the vines into the best shape so they could be the most productive! If this meant drastic pruning, I had to be willing to do so.

A VINEYARD KEEPER MUST HAVE
PATIENCE AND NOT GIVE UP ON HIS
WAYWARD VINES.

Let us not become weary in doing good, for at the proper time we will reap a harvest if we do not give up.

Galatians 6:9

There is the daily tedium of pruning and tying all the new growth. I am very thankful they are growing well, but let's face it...they grow so fast! *(A healthy vine grows about 8-10" in three days during the springtime. Try staying ahead of that kind of growth on 5500 plants!! That's a lot of tying!)* And guess what? Without constant attention, the vines won't continue growing the way I have trained them. If I don't keep tying and training them along the wire, they will grow the wrong way, even if I have tied them several times before. *Will they never learn?*

# A Vineyard Keeper must be selfless.

> Greater love has no one than this, that he lay down his life for his friends.
>
> John 15:13

As the keeper of a vineyard, I must be constantly on guard against anything that would cause harm or damage to my vines: Thieves such as insects or diseases, maybe too much or too little water. Sometimes my husband, Bill, would have to spray fungicide well into the night because of encroaching dangers. He would much rather be in bed but when he knows the situation is urgent, he has no choice! After all, the fruit is in danger!

Bill and I are but poor shadows of *the* Vineyard Keeper. God is our model of love, patience, selflessness and tenacity. And His dealings in our lives are so much like how we deal with our vines. We must daily lay down our lives for our grapevines if we want them to produce a good crop.

# A Vineyard Keeper cares for the well-being of his vineyard.

> But God demonstrates His own love for us in this: While we were still sinners, Christ died for us.
>
> Romans 5:8

As a vineyard keeper, I cannot give up on tying and training the vines though it must be done over and over again, as if they forget it from one week to the next. They will never be perfect. I must be patient with them.

How grateful I am that God does not give up on me as I stumble through life. He did not wait until I was perfect before loving me. If He had, I would never make it. Nor would you, right?

## A VINEYARD KEEPER KNOWS HIS OWN.

> The watchman opens the gate for Him, (the Shepherd) and the sheep listen to His voice. He calls His own sheep by name and leads them out. When He has brought out all His own, He goes on ahead of them, and His sheep follow Him because they know His voice.
>
> John 10:3

As a vineyard keeper, I walk through my field and inspect my plants daily. I *know* my vines; those that are bearing as they should and those that are struggling with disease and /or dying; those that are merely young and immature and those that are weak or damaged. Even in the profusion of weeds around a post (where there appears to be no living vine), if I look closely, I am able to see that one small leaf I know so well. *(I can spot a grape leaf though it is tiny and nearly obscured by the vegetation around it.)* I know *my* vines and I am determined to help them grow and thrive!

# OUR VINEYARD KEEPER IS FAITHFUL!

> If we are faithless, He will remain faithful, for He cannot disown Himself.
>
> 2 Timothy 2:13

Can we trust the One Who holds us in His hand? Is He faithful even when we falter and go astray? 2 Timothy 2:13 is not an excuse to sin, but rather a comforting reminder that we are a part of God; we belong to Him and He will not desert us when we fail. He will keep on keeping on in His love and care for us.

# OUR VINEYARD KEEPER IS PERSISTENT!

> And we know that *in all things* God works for the good of those who love Him, who have been called according to His purpose. (Romans 8:28) italics mine
> "…give thanks in all circumstances, for this is God's will for you in Christ Jesus."
>
> 1 Thessalonians 5:18

We have this assurance: If we willingly put ourselves into the hands of our heavenly Vineyard Keeper, we can know that His *every action in our lives is working for our good*. Every time He prunes us or directs us in a different course, it is for our benefit! Praise the Lord for the reality of these verses. I challenge you to meditate on *your* **very personal** Vineyard Keeper.

# Dead Wood

Did you know that, as a rule, even in the heart of winter when they have no leaves, it is possible to tell a live grapevine from a dead one? When you prune the vine, there is a telltale green in the center of the trunk or shoot. It is also characteristic of healthy, live wood that it is strong and will not break easily. You have to literally cut, not break, any wood you wish to remove...because it is flexible, not brittle.

Often, during the first winter pruning of the season, I approach a vine and wonder if it is alive. To look at this vine on the outside, you might think it was like all the other healthy vines out there...waiting for the springtime to arrive so it can burst into fragrant bloom. However, when I begin to prune it, the wood literally breaks off with just a snap or a twist. Inside, it is brittle and dry and splinters easily. I begin at the top of the vine and proceed downward, cutting the wood to see if there is any indication of life within; all the way down to the ground! If it is not alive, this vine will be removed and replaced. Because the goal of our vineyard is that each vine should *bear much fruit!*

Sometimes, when I look at a plant, it *appears* dead and I am almost certain that I will have to remove it. However, as I proceed with my pruning check, I may get all the way down to the ground and discover just a hint of green in the center. In that case, I will leave the plant; much smaller and pruned back to the ground, but alive! This vine may, in fact, be an older plant previously capable of supporting much fruit; but it will have to go through the whole process of growing and being re-trained before it will again be able to bear fruit. Perhaps disease, insect infestation, or exterior trunk damage has caused it to falter and nearly die. But I, as the Vineyard Keeper, can coax it back to an active, fruitful state over time.

Do you know anyone that used to be on fire for the Lord and was active in service for Him? Then some event derailed them and they became "sick of soul". Or they had a loss that caused them to lose sight of their Savior and mistrust His dealings in their lives. On the outside they may appear to lack any interest in further godly pursuits, to be dead to their faith. But God, *Who looks on the heart*, will find that small ember still burning within. He is able to coax them back into a fruitful relationship with Him by His patient and loving-tender care.

There are also vines that have that "life-like" look. Upon further investigation, however, I discover no evidence of life within. They remind me of some persons who look holy and pious and are involved in all kinds of good works. (Perhaps we wish we could be like them, so busy about the Lord's work!) However, if you get crosswise of them or are unkind to them, they break! They splinter apart! Then we may be the recipients of their unbridled temper; or harsh, biting words may spew from their mouth; or some other ungodly conduct.

What happened? They have a 'form of godliness' but deny the reality of it; they haven't let their faith affect their inward lives. (2 Timothy 3:5) They may be just empty shells simulating Christianity but not having the life of Christ in them. What does Jesus say of this kind of people?

> Not everyone who says to me 'Lord, Lord,' will enter the kingdom of heaven, but only he who does the will of my Father who is in heaven. Many will say to me on that day, 'Lord, Lord, did we not prophesy in your name, and in your name drive out demons, and perform many miracles?' Then I will tell them plainly, 'I never knew you. Away from me, you evildoers!'
>
> Matthew 7:21-23

These are strong words of warning aren't they? It is extremely important to submit ourselves to God. We must establish deep roots in His word, learn His will for us, and discern how to live our lives for Him, not for ourselves. Then we will be able to be effective for Him.

How do we do that? We are told that this is a process, a progression, and does not happen overnight.

For this very reason, make every effort to add to your faith, goodness; and to goodness, knowledge; and to knowledge, self-control; and to self-control, perseverance; and to perseverance, godliness; and to godliness, brotherly kindness; and to brotherly kindness, love. For if you possess these qualities in increasing measure, they will keep you from being ineffective and unproductive in your knowledge of our Lord Jesus Christ.

2 Peter 1:5-8

So get on with it! You have to start somewhere and today is the first day of the rest of your life. Make it count for something eternal! Don't be like the dead wood of a church pew. Be the living, productive wood that is growing and maturing into fruitful service *for His glory*!

# PRUNING

One of my first duties of a new season is the pruning. It is late winter; cold, damp and windy...not at all inviting outside. However, I must make the chilly trek to the vineyard and begin this season's work in the vineyard. Before me are rows of leafless, dormant vines...sleeping until the warm kiss of spring awakens them.

At this same time each year, we begin by pruning off the old wood (branches or shoots from the previous year's growth) in preparation for the new growth of the season. We prune off all old wood from each vertical shoot, leaving only two new buds. Each horizontal branch (called a cordon) is shortened according to the age and health of the plant. If I do not perform this crucial step, the vines will produce buds along the entire length of the branches and trunk; each bud will, in turn, produce two clusters of grapes. What, you may ask (as I did) is the matter with that? Isn't more fruit better? Not necessarily. Over-fruiting, as it is called, will result in depleting the vine of valuable reserves. This results in poorer quality of fruit next year, and if this pattern is continued it can cause early "burn-out" of the vine.

Therefore, I must train myself not to look at the quantity of previous growth but at the age and maturity of each individual plant. If too many buds are left on the vine, the plant will not be able to adequately support all of the resulting fruit. When the vine is pruned properly, it is able to support this year's growth and store adequate resources for the year to come. The vine continues its maturing process as it sends its roots down deeper into the earth where its nutrients and water are...its very life! Each year of proper training encourages the vine along a prescribed course. (You see, the root system below ground must be greater than the growth above ground.) Consequently, the older, mature vines are able to nourish more fruit than the baby vines (because they have deeper roots and better resources to draw upon).

Jesus spoke of this important pruning process.

> I am the true Vine, and my Father is the gardener. He cuts off every branch in me that bears no fruit, while every branch that does bear fruit He prunes so that it will be even more fruitful.

> John 15:1-2

It is vital, as a Christian, to willingly submit to our Father's pruning process so that we will be able to mature. Only then will we be able to understand deeper truths of God and store up the needed strength to withstand the trials and temptations that *will* come. Paul addresses this need for maturity in his letter to the Corinthians.

> Brothers, I could not address you as spiritual but as worldly–mere infants in Christ. I gave you milk, not solid food, for you were not yet ready for it. Indeed, you are still not ready.

1 Corinthians 3:1-2

As a Christian studies the Bible daily and learns to discern God's mind and ways, he matures and pushes his roots down deep into these truths, leaving the wisdom of the world behind. This gives him stability and maturity to handle the responsibilities and the many challenges that will come or any resulting acclaim he may receive.

There may be times when God does not allow us to pursue a desired course...or He says "*no*" to more church activities and busy-ness "*for Him*". It may be that we need more time to mature and develop deeper roots in His word in order to withstand the winds of adversity that He knows will come. Only when He sees we are ready, will He bring greater opportunities to be of service; both to Him and His body, the Church. Christ says:

> Remain in me, and I will remain in you. No branch can bear fruit by itself. Neither can you bear fruit unless you remain in me.

John 15:4

Remember our fruit comes only from association with Him (Jesus). Any fruit we produce on our own is of no use to Him. His goal is to train us in such a way that we are most fruitful *for the kingdom of God*. That is why He spends so much time and effort on us! If He didn't care, we would be left to ourselves; like a wild grapevine that grows in all directions, producing lots of visible fruit, but without any real value. (A wild grapevine produces so much fruit that it does not have the high quality we are looking for. It appears good, but we don't want to use it. Quality is definitely better than quantity.)

Admittedly, this pruning process in our lives is painful, isn't it? But James says there is a reason for us to find joy in and patiently endure the trials and frustrations of this life. These **tribulations produce the best fruit**, fruit that is of great value in the kingdom of heaven!

> Consider it pure joy, my brothers, whenever you face trials of many kinds, because you know that the testing of your faith develops perseverance. Perseverance must finish its work so that you may be mature and complete, not lacking anything.
>
> James 1:2-4

So take heart. God is pruning you to be the best you can be! Isn't it encouraging that He cares so much? Willingly submit to Him and see what a beautiful, abundantly fruitful Christian you can become.

# UNEVEN GROWTH

As I stroll through the vineyard, I often see something that puzzles me. My grapevines do not all grow at the same rate. Though they were planted at the *same time*, in the *same field* (a mere 8' from one another), receiving the *same sun*, *same fertilizer*, *same soil*, etc. their size can vary greatly! Presumably, there are no differences that can account for one vine growing very strong and fast, and another barely surviving.

Yet there it is. I have one plant that is ready to bear a good crop of fruit this season…and eight feet away there is another vine that is small and skinny, with little growth since it was planted three years ago. As a matter of fact, just looking at the smaller vine I may be prepared to cut it back severely, or even remove it. But when I test the vine I find life!

First, let's review the essential ingredients necessary to grow healthy, productive grapevines. *Good soil, fertilizer, weed-free environment, water, sunlight and good pest control.* Upon closer examination I may find that the drip emitter above the pitiful, little plant is stopped up. And, of course, without water this vine has had very little chance of growing to maturity and bearing fruit.

Or it could be there are weeds crowding around the base of this poor, under-grown plant. Maybe we waited too long to get rid of them and they have taken their toll. *(Weeds compete mercilessly for available water and food from the soil.)* If there has been too little water, then weeds could entirely account for the differences. The smaller plant may be alive, but just barely!

So here's an application. Do you know someone who professed to have love and faith in Jesus Christ years before? They 'walked the aisle' but have seldom, if ever, darkened the door to the church since. Perhaps they have a Bible, but it is gathering dust, not being used for study and growth. Since they have been cut off from the "Living Water", they have not grown in their faith.

Possibly, they have been submersing themselves in the ungodly influences of this world (the weeds) which are choking any spiritual life from them! No wonder there is no visible, spiritual fruit. It does not matter that they may be a success in the World's eyes; in the end, *they can take none of their works or their money with them!* On Judgment Day they will appear to *The Judge* as pitiful as that small, fruitless vine does to me...dead! It is possible they are truly 'saved', but they will have no rewards in heaven. Consider these sobering words.

> If any man builds on this foundation (Jesus Christ) using gold, silver, costly stones, wood, hay or straw, his work will be shown for what it is, because the Day will bring it to light. It will be revealed with fire, and the fire will test the quality of each man's work. If what he has built survives, he will receive his reward. If it is burned up, he will suffer loss; he himself will be saved, but only as one escaping through the flames.
>
> 1 Corinthians 3:12-15

On the other hand, let's look at the mature, healthy vine that is ready to bear fruit. This vine has had a relatively weed-free environment. (He has kept himself unstained by the world.) It has been steadily pumping a plentiful supply of water up into to its branches. (Through Bible study and prayer.) The result is visible (fruit of the Spirit), as well as the unseen, (deep roots that carry him through the difficulties in his life).

In our own lives, we must be tapped into *the* Source of life; and through our roots, Christ will cause His life to be pumped into us. This in turn can't help but result in outward growth and fruit that is evident to anyone who cares to look. Each person's fruit will not be the same, but <u>it will be visible</u>. So much Life will be flowing through us that the Vineyard Keeper will have to prune (or direct) us regularly because of our zeal to be busy about His work. Otherwise, we might become over-committed, shooting out in all directions in our exuberance for Him and His kingdom.

This should be our goal. Fruitfulness! There is no shortcut to maturity. It takes years, it takes study, and it takes prayer. It also takes a willingness to submit to the Master's plan for our life, even though it is contrary to our own goals. Luke states the importance of following hard after our Lord.

> If any one would come after me, he must deny himself and take up his cross daily and follow me. For whoever wants to save his life will lose it, but whoever loses his life for me will save it. What good is it for a man to gain the whole world, and yet lose or forfeit his very self?

> Luke 9:23-25

Again we see the parallels. We cannot grow to maturity and productivity without our *Source of life*. **He** is our reason for *being* and our reason for *growing*. My prayer for you, as well as myself, is this

> ...(That) you may be mature and complete, lacking nothing.

> James 1:4b

# Oh, The Fragrance!

It's the end of winter at last and the whole earth seems to be singing! Spring signals her coming by warming the earth and air, stimulating new leaves and wildflowers, green grass, etc. Birds are singing and new life is evident everywhere! Spring has come!

Our grapevines are busy pumping life from their roots into their trunks and branches, gearing up for their growing season. Every bud is soft and full, literally bursting with glorious potential! The buds will soon send out shoots of miniature green leaves; and then they will produce exquisite, aromatic blossoms that look like a tiny cluster of grapes. Amazingly enough, each cluster of blooms smells like the variety of grapes they will produce. The fragrance is heavenly! The blooms must then be pollinated in order for the fruit to begin growing. (God has provided bees for this job.)

Did you know the Bible says we as Christians have a smell? We have the fragrance of life because of our association with Jesus Christ. Paul put it like this:

> For we are to God the aroma of Christ among those
> who are being saved and those who are perishing. To
> the one we are the smell of death; to the other, the
> fragrance of life.
>
> 2 Corinthians 2:15

How marvelous! We smell like our Savior! And just as
the grape blossoms need pollination, we, as believers, need
others involved in our lives to increase our effectiveness.
Some may not think it necessary to be involved in a local
body of believers (commonly referred to as a church), but
we are not left to live this life alone. Fellow Christians can
encourage and exhort us, and challenge us to be more like
our Master; much like the bees pollinate our grape blooms.

The Bible is full of illustrations of the power and
importance of the "church" or "body". We are not alone,
we are to work in concert with our brothers and sisters
in Christ.

> ...We are all members of one body.
>
> Ephesians 4:25

> Let us not give up meeting together, as some are in
> the habit of doing, but let us encourage one another.
>
> Hebrews 10:25

Now let's get personal. Do you accept the suggestions and exhortations of fellow believers who truly desire to help you? Are you accountable to at least one other believer who will help you stay true to God's standards? Do you strive to do the same for them? Or are you the "Lone Ranger" trying to do it all yourself?

How *do* you smell? Do you have the fragrance of life or the stench of death? Do you have any fragrance at all? Are you so 'generic' that no one would be able to identify you or know to Whom you belong? (This state of being is commonly referred to as being a "worldly Christian".) We are really supposed to be conduits (channels) for the Lord.

> ...Through us spreads everywhere the fragrance of the knowledge of Him.
>
> 2 Corinthians 2:14

We are purveyors of God's message to a sick and sad world...His fragrance of love if you will. We have been entrusted with the responsibility of representing Christ to all those around us. Paul, in the book of Romans, poses the question:

> How, then, can they call on the One they have not believed in? And how can they believe in the One of whom they have not heard? And how can they hear without someone preaching to them?
>
> Romans 10:14

*Deanna L. Martin*

Another characteristic fragrance of Christians is supposed to be our love for one another. 1 Corinthians 13, the "love chapter", lists qualities that should be evident in every believer's life. These attributes are not typical qualities people are striving after in the world. Modern society teaches a "me first", "grab all the gusto you can get", "you only go around once" attitude. But just look at all the unhappy, unfulfilled, empty people in the world. Completely different from Jesus' life and teaching, isn't it? Real happiness comes from unselfish giving, as we read in the following.

> Love is patient, love is kind. It does not envy, it does not boast, it is not proud. It is not rude, it is not self-seeking, it is not easily angered, it keeps no record of wrongs. Love does not delight in evil but rejoices with the truth. It always protects, always trusts, always hopes, always perseveres. Love never fails.
>
> 1 Corinthians 13:4-8a

Let's face it...we have been given quite an assignment (and privilege) as God's messengers on earth! Jesus modeled the servant-life while He walked the earth and His word (the Bible) lays it out for us in black and white. First and foremost you must make sure you are tapped into the "True Vine" or you cannot bear genuine Christ-like fruit. Let's strive to be the loveliest "perfume" of the Lord exhibiting the hope and joy of the Lord that others are so desperately seeking. And let it become our goal to be sweet-smelling "air fresheners" wherever we go, always ready to tell them where we get that wonderful fragrance!

# Pests and Diseases!

Gnats, mosquitoes, flies, crickets, spiders, grasshoppers...
PESTS! Hasn't everyone been annoyed by these common,
aggravating critters? (*I sometimes find it difficult to stay out
and work when these pests are flying all around my head and
landing on my face, arms, etc. Makes you wonder why they
were created, doesn't it?*) Even certain species of lovely birds
can become pests in our vineyard.

As in any agricultural venture we have to be vigilant
against all pests in the vineyard. Some insects can devour
the leaves on our vines, taking away their ability to grow;
some devour our ripening fruit; and some can kill the whole
vine by infecting it with disease!

Grasshoppers, for example, can eat so many of the
leaves on the vines that the plants may be barely able to
survive, their fruit cannot ripen or they may even die. And
as harvest nears and the grapes begin to get sweet, some
birds descend and eat as much fruit as they can (which is
a lot). Some moths, too, love the fruit as it ripens. They
poke holes in the grapes and drain the juice thereby ruining
them. And then there are Japanese beetles. They are lovely
to look at with their iridescent colored backs but left
unhindered, they can destroy the entire crop...right before

Deanna L. Martin

harvest! Thankfully, we have some preventative measures we can take. Usually we can spray for these pests and be reasonably free of them.

Then, there is a disease called "Blackrot". This is a devastating fungus found in the more humid parts of the country. This fungus begins on the leaves of the vines and, if left untreated, spreads to the fruit. When the temperature is above 80 degrees and it is extremely humid or it rains, the bacterium begins growing.

The fungus begins as small chocolate-colored spots on the leaves and begins to grow and multiply. Then it progresses to the fruit. If it is not stopped, it can destroy the crop and turn all the grapes to hard, black "mummies" in just a matter of three weeks time. These "mummies" are of no value at all. We have seen an entire forty-acre vineyard destroyed by Blackrot because proper steps were not taken to stop it. A critical responsibility of the vineyard keeper is to be on the look out for Blackrot.

There is one deadly adversary that attacks our vineyard that we can do little to prevent and nothing to get rid of, once we have been infected by it. It is known as Pierces disease. An insect known as a sharpshooter carries this devastating disease and will insert his long, sucker-like mouth all the way into the inmost part (the xylem) of the unsuspecting vine. In this simple way the vine becomes infected with the deadly bacteria. The insects can go from vine to vine and infect the entire vineyard. Many vineyards have been destroyed in this way!

The only known defense against Pierce's Disease is a very cold winter. It is believed that when the temperatures drop below freezing for a minimum of 1000-1200 hours during the winter that the prolonged cold temperatures kill the bacteria within the plant, even after it is infected. This prevents the spread to other healthy vines as well as stopping the disease from further destroying the infected vine. The outcome, however, is not in our hands, as you can tell, since we do not control the weather.

Similarly, there are pests in our spiritual lives; pests we call sins. Some sins seem minor to us and, like pests, they annoy us by their persistent temptations. Just when we think we have a handle on that "sin that so easily besets us" here it comes again! There are many of these "small" sins referred to in the Bible. (*Of course, Jesus does not think of any sin as minor. That is a human invention.*)

> ...Be on your guard against the yeast of the Pharisees, which is hypocrisy.
>
> Luke 12:1b

The dictionary defines hypocrisy as "pretending to be what one is not". Is there any hypocrisy in your life? Do you say one thing and do another? (Our children, spouse or best friend can be a good judge of this.) This is a sneaky pest that may seem insignificant but we all need to take measures against this sneaky *pest*.

How about that little trespass referred to as greed (defined as "excessive desire")?

> Watch out! Be on your guard against all kinds of greed; a man's life does not consist in the abundance of his possessions.
>
> Luke 12:15

Do your material possessions occupy their rightful place in your heart? (Like...near the bottom of your priorities list?) Material possessions, or the pursuit of such, can really hinder us if they hold too tight a grip on our heart. Like pests, they can rob us of the godly fruit we desire to produce. Matthew reminds us what our priorities should be.

> Seek first His kingdom and His righteousness and all these things will be given to you as well.
>
> Matthew 6:33

Then there are much more sinister sins that mirror Pierces Disease and infect us down into the very marrow of our bones. (*You know what I mean.*) A few examples are alcoholism, drug abuse, gambling, lust, pornography, sexual sin, etc. Each one starts out innocently, with just a simple little "sting of the insect". But these are deadly vices and they can get such a hold on us that we begin to die spiritually, dragging down our loved ones with us. As arrogant humans, we think we can flirt with sin but turn at the last minute and be fine. However, since our sinful natures tend toward sin anyway, we are more likely to be ensnared when temptation comes our way. We need to FLEE when temptation knocks and recognize the danger of giving it *any* foothold in our lives.

> Flee from sexual immorality. All other sins a person commits are outside the body, but whoever sins sexually, sins against their own body.
>
> 1 Corinthians 6:18

> Turn from evil and do good, seek peace and pursue it.
>
> Psalm 34:14

> But you, man of God, flee from all this, and pursue righteousness, godliness, faith, love, endurance and gentleness.
>
> 1 Timothy 6:11

How do we prevent the deadly diseases of our sinful nature from taking hold of us and killing our spirit? Colossians gives directions for staying pure.

> Set your minds on things above, not on earthly things. For you died and your life is now hidden with Christ in God. Put to death, therefore, whatever belongs to your earthly nature: sexual immorality, impurity, lust, evil desires and greed, which is idolatry.
>
> Colossians 3:2,5

And listen to this word of urgent warning that rings out in Hebrews.

> If we deliberately keep on sinning after we have received the knowledge of the truth, no sacrifice for sins is left.
>
> Hebrews 10:26

Fearful words, are they not? As in any other area, God has not left us to ourselves in this matter. Here is His wonderful promise to His children!

> My grace is sufficient for you, for my power is made perfect in weakness.
>
> 2 Corinthians 12:6

There are so many things Satan uses in our lives to pester us and rob us of the joy, victory and peace that are ours in Christ Jesus. His desire is to get us to take our eyes off of the Lord and look to *things* to satisfy and bring fulfillment.

But press on! Watch out! Be on your guard! And take heed to a final challenge from the apostle Paul found in Ephesians:

> "I urge you to live a life worthy of the calling you have received."
>
> Ephesians 4:1

# Meditation Nine
# WEEDS!

Are there weeds in your garden? What about in your beautifully manicured lawn? If there aren't, is it because you just happen to have one of those plots of ground that do not give sanctuary to these exasperating vegetations? I think not! If you do not have weeds, it is because you have worked very hard to get rid of them, right? There is not a place on God's earth where you do not have to continually fight to keep the weed population from taking over your spot of ground. (Outside of the Garden of Eden, that is!)

Weeds present an enormous problem for us in the vineyard, especially the Johnson grass! All year long we engage in all out war against them. Why? Because one thing becomes evident when you are comparing growth and productivity of the grapevines to one another. One critical factor is the number and size of weeds that inhabit the same space with the vines. The weeds literally rob the vines of nutrients and water, as well as block out the sun that is vital for them to thrive. It is an either/or situation; either the weeds will win or the vines, not both! They cannot exist in the same space without some measure of detriment to the vines.

Oddly enough, the weeds rarely lose the battle without help from us, especially with the smaller vines! If the grapevine is large enough it is able to fend off destruction with fewer noticeable effects. However the small, immature plants show the strain quickly if they have to continually compete with the ravenous weed population for their daily sustenance. In areas where the Johnson grass is left unhindered, it may grow 8-10' high. Our poor little vine may be a mere 15" tall.

In areas where weed control is actively practiced, you will see a vine of the same age has grown 4' tall with an abundance of leaves and small shoots. Its trunk may be four or five times thicker than the one surrounded by the tall, choking weeds.

Sunlight is another essential for healthy growth of the vines. The process of converting sunlight into food for the plant is known as photosynthesis. Water is the transportation system used by the vine to transport the nutrition derived from the soil, distributing it from the tiniest root tips all the way to the leaf tips. It is a wonderfully designed system by the Master, Himself! Without this process, the plant will not be able to obtain and utilize everything it needs to reach maturity and begin bearing fruit.

In much the same way, pests (sins) will hinder our growth as Christians. Weeds can do serious damage, as well. "Weeds" (personal sins) in our lives can keep us from living effective lives for Christ. Jesus describes what happens with weeds in the parable of the sower, found in Matthew. The farmer sowed his seeds in several different locations, one of which was among weeds (thorns).

> A farmer went out to sow his seed. As he was scattering the seed, some fell along the path, and the birds came and ate it up. Some fell on rocky places, where it did not have much soil. It sprang up quickly, because the soil was shallow. But when the sun came up, the plants were scorched, and they withered because they had no root. Other seed fell among thorns, which grew up and choked the plants. Still other seed fell on good soil, where it produced a crop-a hundred, sixty or thirty times what was sown.
>
> Matthew 13:1-8

There are varied circumstances that can prevent us from accepting the word of *truth* and acting on it which He described in his story. Later in the passage, He continues with an explanation of what it means to be a Christian surrounded by weeds.

> The one who received the seed that fell among the thorns is the man who hears the word, but the worries of this life and the deceitfulness of wealth choke it, making it unfruitful.
>
> Matthew 13:22

He does not say that the Christian living among the weeds is not a believer, but that he is unfruitful. The fruitful believer is represented, in that same parable, as the seed that fell on good soil.

> But the one who received the seed that fell on good soil is the man who hears the word and understands it. He produces a crop, yielding a hundred, sixty or thirty times what was sown.
>
> Matthew 13:23

So...what is *our crop* supposed to be, anyway? I know that a grapevine will produce **grapes** since l*ike* produces *like*. This is a very basic principle of life from the beginning of time.

> "My brothers, can a fig tree bear olives, or a grapevine bear figs?"
>
> James 3:12

As Christians, we have been grafted onto "The Vine", which is Jesus Christ. To be grafted means that we were surgically taken from our original nature (by the cross) and supernaturally implanted into the body of Christ (by Christ's triumph over the grave). We are no longer slaves to the old nature of sin but are free to partake of the new nature of Jesus. And as part of our new nature in Christ, we are to bear fruit in keeping with that new association.

Spiritual fruit such as compassion, mercy, forgiveness, gratefulness, servant-hood, love to our fellow man, etc.

I believe it is time we as Christians do some serious weeding in our lives? **Be bold!** Ask God to show you where you have allowed Satan to choke the life from within you? (*The life of Jesus in you, I mean.*) Take an honest inventory. Remember…whatever interferes with and/or supersedes our devotion to God is instantaneously a hindrance to *His* life presence flowing through us.

MEDITATION TEN

# SHOOTS AND CORDONS

A very important part of training the vines involves deciding which shoots should be left to grow upright, which should become the cordon, and which should be removed altogether. This is very important because each shoot that is left to grow will require food and energy. We must channel all growth in the direction we want it to go or it will divert valuable resources and become a drain on the plant. Several scenarios present themselves in this regard as a vineyard keeper surveys his vines.

There are three levels of wire on each row. When a new vine grows from the ground and finally reaches the main (or middle) wire it has many shoots growing upwards. The vineyard keeper must determine which two shoots are strongest (one on either side) and prune off the others. These two shoots will then be tied horizontally on to the wire to form the cordons. These will be the base for the upward growing shoots. The strength of the cordon determines the strength of its shoots and, consequently, the quality of fruit. As the cordon grows along the cordon wire, we leave one upward-growing shoot every three to four inches. These shoots become the fruit-bearing vessels.

Here is the next important principle shown in the cordon. The shoot that forms the cordon will not, itself, bear fruit. There will be no glory for the cordon; it will be the base structure only. The vine cannot reach maximum production of fruit if there is not a strong cordon supporting all the fruit-bearing shoots.

Similarly, in the body of Christ, we find that God has gifted different people for different jobs. There are a lot of behind-the-scenes support people who make the Body (church) function properly. These background workers do not get the glory and acclaim of standing before a congregation preaching an eloquent sermon. They are not the ones who sing an inspiring song that lifts the listener's hearts to heaven.

They are those who teach the little ones in Sunday School and Choir; who take care of our toddlers so we will not be distracted while we go to our classes and to "big church". How about those who clean the church so the rest of us can worship in a clean sanctuary? And the church secretaries that take care of daily office work. The list could go on, couldn't it? We all know dear people who are willing to give of their time and energy, at any time, to help someone in need, without fanfare or reward? They are people who work quietly for the Lord without any recognition from others. They are doing it for their Master.

The fact is that our pastor, music director and youth pastor would not be able to perform their jobs as ably if it weren't for the supporting servants. Scripture teaches that each believer is given a different role (or gift) in the Body of Christ. Each is equally important, though not all receive the same acclaim and notoriety here on earth. There is, however, one Source of all of our abilities

> There are different kinds of gifts, but the same Spirit. There are different kinds of service, but the same Lord. There are different kinds of working, but the same God works all of them in all men. Now to each one the manifestation of the Spirit is given for the common good.
>
> 1 Corinthians 12:4-7

Another area of training that is absolutely *crucial* for the growing vine involves ridding the plant of "suckers" and "bull shoots". Throughout the growing season, the vineyard keeper must be vigilant to prune off all the shoots that try to grow along the trunk of the vine or from underneath the cordons. A little shoot, or 'sucker' (as they are aptly named) growing on the trunk below the cordons will become a "bull shoot" if allowed to grow unhindered. They can become very thick and long with lots of lush foliage…because they are siphoning off the nutrients coming from the roots. But they seldom bear any fruit. All of their energy is put into that tremendous, showy, green growth. Again, no fruit!

I have observed some Christians who remind me of 'bull shoots'. They are working so hard "for the Lord" that they are too busy to spend time with Him and find out if they are doing the things *He* thinks are important. And you know they are too busy to for their families. But when you check for the 'Fruit of the Spirit' listed in Galatians, you won't find it in their lives.

> But the fruit of the Spirit is love, joy, peace, patience, kindness, goodness, faithfulness, gentleness and self-control. Against such things there is no law.
>
> Galatians 5:22-23

These people are often working for the praise of man and not for the glory of their Lord. Take heed. We are told that God looks upon the heart, not at our outward works. What does He see in your heart? In my heart? Does He see a servant's heart? Does He see love for our fellow believers? Or simply a cold, hard heart that is interested only in the accolades of men? It is never too late to get ourselves right with our Maker. He, and only He, is the One Who can give us a new tender heart that is concerned with the things about which He is concerned, regardless of what others think.

*Father, give us a servant's heart that we may be willing to lay down our lives in service to You, without thought of what others may think!*

# MEDITATION ONE

## THE DREAM

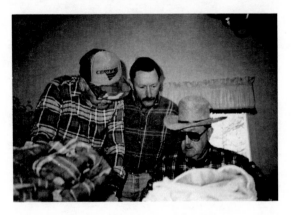

Operation--Martin Vineyard

# MEDITATION TWO

## Changing Seasons

Winter (...So very important to the grapevines)

Spring

Summer (...hot, humid and dry in Texas!)

Autumn

# MEDITATION THREE

## VINEYARD KEEPER

# MEDITATION FOUR
## DEAD WOOD

# MEDITATION FIVE
## PRUNING

# MEDITATION SIX
## UNEVEN GROWTH

# MEDITATION SEVEN
## OH, THE FRAGRANCE!

# MEDITATION EIGHT
## PESTS AND DISEASES!

# MEDITATION NINE
## WEEDS!

# MEDITATION TEN
## SHOOTS AND CORDONS

# MEDITATION ELEVEN
## TENDRILS AND TIES

# MEDITATION TWELVE

## FRUIT!

# MEDITATION THIRTEEN

## GREENHOUSE EFFECT

# MEDITATION FOURTEEN
## HARVEST!

# MEDITATION FIFTEEN
## DEVASTATION!

# MEDITATION SIXTEEN
## LETTING GO

# MEDITATION SEVENTEEN
## BLACKROT!

# MEDITATION EIGHTEEN

## PLAGUE

# MEDITATION NINETEEN

## BOUNTEOUS HARVEST!

# MEDITATION TWENTY
## MUSTARD SEED

# MEDITATION TWENTY-ONE
## LAST STRAW

# Epilogue

# THE END ...
# AND NEW BEGINNING?

# TENDRILS AND TIES

I am fascinated by another very cool phenomenon I see in the vineyard: **tendrils**. Tendrils are curly, green "fingers" that grow out from the upward shoots on the vines and catch onto anything within their reach. They do this in order to steady themselves in the wind. These tiny tendrils seem delicate, yet they have tremendous strength. The uppermost wire is called the "catch" wire. As its name implies, it is there so the upward growing shoots can catch on so they do not break-off during strong winds.

We use green vinyl tie tape to manually secure the shoots to the catch wire. This procedure serves two purposes: (1) to help keep shoots upright, allowing the fruit on the vine to be exposed to the sunlight as it hangs freely below, and (2) to help prevent breakage of the shoots when the wind blows hard (which is very common in our area).

However, with all the other responsibilities I have to do in tending the vineyard, this operation frequently does not get done on a timely basis. As usual, God has His own way of solving this dilemma and protecting the vines at the same time.

I remember being amazed the first time I saw a tender, green tendril wrapped around the catch wire. I asked what it was doing and why. My patient husband-teacher explained that this was nature's way of tying the vine to the wire for stability. The tendril seemed fragile, but when I tried to pull it, it did not come loose easily. As a matter of fact, it was quite difficult to get loose. And I learned that the longer it stays wrapped around something, the stronger it becomes… eventually becoming wood. Bill told me that whenever a breeze kicks up, this wind action *actually stimulates* the vine to put out these little feelers and wrap around whatever is closest to them. They wrap round and round several times to anchor the shoot securely. *It does not happen on calm days!* Tendril production occurs only during windy times. The stronger the wind, the faster these little "fingers" grab on and the stronger they become! They will even grab onto a tall weed if it is handy, or the drip wire, or another part of the vine, itself, even if it causes them to grow in the wrong direction. They are looking for anything that can bring stability to their windy world. (Sound familiar?)

When circumstances in our life are calm and pleasant, human tendency is to be unaware of our need of God. I know in peaceful times I am tempted to try and live in my own strength. I temporarily forget how crucial God is in my life. My Bible study time may become less important and my prayers less than frequent. However, when the winds of adversity begin to blow and I am in distress, I sure do cry out to God urgently and reach out for Him. It is during these times that I am very aware that I cannot withstand the onslaught of circumstances in my own strength!

The Psalms are full of people crying out to God in desperate need and their blessed assurance that He has heard them and will come to their aid.

> When I was in great need, He saved me.
>
> Psalm 116:6

> In my anguish I cried to the Lord, and He answered by setting me free.
>
> Psalm 118:5

> When my spirit grows faint within me, it is You who know my way.
>
> Psalm 142:3

*It is this awareness of our great need that draws us to God.* Those of us who have known grievous sorrow and tremendous tragedy know the deep comfort of the Lord during that time; much more than when our life was rocking gently along. I realize that during these times in my own life, when I felt as if I could not carry on, the Lord had "tied" me to Him.

How *inestimable* was the comfort to my soul, knowing that my Lord had secured me to Himself and that He would not let me go, even when my strength was so very small. I will never forget His tender, loving comfort during these times. And because I have been so comforted, I am better able to relate to and comfort others in need. The following verse has been a wonderful reminder to me that God takes even our misfortunes and uses them to His glory and for the benefit of others.

> Who (*God*) comforts us in all our troubles, so that we can comfort those in any trouble with the comfort we ourselves have received from God.
>
> 2 Corinthians 1:4

It is important to remember that the trials and temptations remind us of our need for God. They are working His purposes in our lives and better help us relate to others who need comforting. Perhaps you recall the song lyric that said, "If I'd never had a problem, I wouldn't know that God could solve them."

And knowing that we tend to become frustrated and discouraged with the trials in our lives, Paul reminds us that God has a purpose and is actually using them.

> Consider it pure joy, my brothers, whenever you face trials of many kinds, because you know that the testing of your faith develops perseverance.
>
> James 1:2-3

To drive the concept home, how are we to look at our hardships (in light of eternity)?

> I consider that our present sufferings are not worth comparing with the glory that will be revealed in us.
>
> Romans 8:18

We have got to remember these trials are only temporary. Our life is short on this earth. Someday we will be with Jesus and all sad memories will fade away.

> He will wipe every tear from their eyes. There will be no more death or mourning or crying or pain, for the old order of things has passed away.

> Revelation 21:4

What a promise! So forget the grumbling and complaining. Make sure that whatever you are holding onto for security is not a "weed", but the everlasting Creator of the Universe. And hold onto this...that when all of your strength is gone, **He'll never let go of you**. His "ties" to us are indestructible through Jesus Christ. Praise His Holy Name!

# Fruit!

When we began this wild adventure of growing grapes, we had a specific goal in mind. That goal was (and always will be) to raise healthy vines that would produce high quality grapes for years to come. We set our minds to know all that was involved in this process and how to be successful at it. As in any other worthwhile enterprise, it takes a lot of time and effort to reach the goal.

The same holds true for the Christian life. Our goal should be to live a life that is pleasing to the Lord and bears fruit that is pleasing to Him. Lasting fruit can only be produced when we are attached to the True Vine. We are given a summary of spiritual fruit in Galatians. This is fruit that *will be produced* when we are rightly connected with God. We spoke of this before, but it bears repeating!

> The fruit of the Spirit is love, joy, peace, patience, kindness, goodness, faithfulness, gentleness, and self-control. Against such things there is no law.
>
> Galatians 5:22-23

We should not deceive ourselves; God *does notice* and *cares deeply* about the quality of fruit we bear. As a matter of fact, we see that each of us *is* bearing fruit, good or bad, and that it is evident to all who see us.

> No good tree bears bad fruit, nor does a bad tree bear good fruit. Each tree is recognized by its own fruit. People do not pick figs from thorn bushes, or grapes from briers. The good man brings good things out of the good stored up in his heart, and the evil man brings evil things out of the evil stored up in his heart. For out of the overflow of his heart his mouth speaks.
>
> Luke 6:43-45

As a season progresses toward harvest, we examine the plants regularly, inspecting the fruit. The fruit each vine produces tells us a lot about the plant itself. We can tell if we have left too much fruit on the vine for it to ripen properly. Maybe the shoots have not grown long enough or have too few leaves to support the number of clusters on that shoot. Are the grapes fully developing, or are some clusters much smaller than others on the same vine? Are they ripening evenly with even coloring, or are there unripe green grapes mixed in with the ripe ones?

The answers to these questions are important in helping us determine what each vine is capable of handling. Some problems tell us the plant will need to be re-trained next season in order to increase its overall health. We must maintain a delicate balance between foliage and fruit production. In order to get the maximum quality of fruit from the vine, you must have the foliage needed to feed it throughout the season (*someone, somewhere, actually counted how many leaves are needed per cluster. It's 22!*). If you have too much foliage, it will not set as much fruit as it is capable of producing; and most of the energy of the plant will go to its leaves. It is up to the vineyard keeper to correct any deficiencies and help bring the plant into balance.

The same holds true for the Christian. Paul tells us that a mature Christian should evidence certain qualities that are apparent to an observer.

> And we pray this in order that you may live a life worthy of the Lord and may please Him in every way: bearing fruit in every good work, growing in the knowledge of God, being strengthened with all power according to His glorious might so that you may have great endurance and patience, and joyfully giving thanks to the Father, Who has qualified you to share in the inheritance of the saints in the kingdom of light. For He has rescued us from the dominion of darkness and brought us into the kingdom of the Son He loves, in Whom we have redemption, the forgiveness of sins.
>
> Colossians 1:10

And James reminds us that believers are to be character-ized by the following:

> But the wisdom that comes from heaven is first of all pure; then peace-loving, considerate, submissive, full of mercy and good fruit, impartial and sincere. Peacemakers who sow in peace raise a harvest of righteousness.
>
> James 3:17

These "fruits" are rare in our contemporary worldly society because most people are not connected to the same *Vine* we are! This is why it is so very important that we as God's representatives to the World, exhibit godly qualities. We have been chosen to bear fruit so that the unbelieving world around us will see it and be attracted to **HIM**! Then they will be able to see that there is a better way to live; and that joy and peace can be theirs even in this troubling world. John tells us that we have been chosen by the Most High God for a very specific reason...to bear fruit!

> You did not choose me, but I chose you and appointed you to go and bear fruit–fruit that will last. Then the Father will give you whatever you ask in my name. This is my command: Love each other.
>
> John 15:16

Again we are told that we do not belong to ourselves. Our association with Christ is intended to produce a distinctive fruit!

> So, my brothers, you also died to the law through the body of Christ, that you might belong to another, to Him Who was raised from the dead, in order that we might bear fruit to God.
>
> Romans 7:4

Another result of being rightly related to God is righteousness (or moral virtue)...a quality that is sorely lacking in our world today! This is a quality that yields a precious, rare fruit.

> The fruit of righteousness will be peace.
>
> Isaiah 32:17

Everyone is looking for peace! They try to legislate it, teach it in the school curriculum (*teaching tolerance of everyone's personal agendas*) and even try to force peace through wars! Christians have been given the formula and we should be shouting it from the rooftops!

Okay, so now the practical application of all of this. Maybe you *say* you are a Christian but there is none of the distinctive fruit we have just been describing in your life. You are in a dangerous position. Jesus had this to say about you.

> The axe is already at the root of the trees, and every tree that does not produce good fruit will be cut down and thrown into the fire.
>
> Matthew 3:10

He does not care about what you speak so much as the reality of your heart. By the way, just *how* are you to prove your Christianity if there are no outward signs? The apostle Paul posed this question.

> What good is it, my brothers, it a man claims to have faith but has no deeds? Can such faith save him? Suppose a brother or sister is without clothes and daily food. If one of you says to him, "Go, I wish you well; keep warm and well fed," but does nothing about his physical needs, what good is it? In the same way, faith by itself, if it is not accompanied by action, is dead...Show me your faith without deeds, and I will show you my faith by what I do.
>
> James 2:14-18

The time has come for us to seriously examine our lives in light of the scriptures, not just our religious traditions. Since the goal of the Christian life is to bear fruit, we had better...*that's right*, check our fruit! Better yet, ask someone else to evaluate your fruit. Are you producing the true "fruit of the Spirit" that evidences Christ's life within you? If not, check your connection to "The Vine". He is ready and willing to supply His life to you so that you may be truly productive. As believers, we have a precious promise found in the Old Testament book of Jeremiah.

> He will be like a tree planted by the water that sends out its roots by the stream. It does not fear when heat comes; its leaves are always green. It has no worries in a year of drought and never fails to bear fruit.

> Jeremiah 17:8

The *"He"* in that verse refers to us, God's beloved children. Again, nothing worth having comes easily in this life and growing in maturity takes work and time, but the benefits are well worth the effort. I found what I'll call a Christian "To Do" list that encourages us to press on and not give up!

> For this very reason, make every effort to add to your faith goodness; and to goodness, knowledge; and to knowledge, self-control; and to self-control, perseverance; and to perseverance, godliness; and to godliness, brotherly kindness; and to brotherly kindness, love. For if you possess these qualities in increasing measure, they will keep you from being ineffective and unproductive in your knowledge of our Lord Jesus Christ.

> 2 Peter 1:5-8

So don't give up. Keep pressing on. The rewards are well worth the effort!

## Meditation Thirteen
# Greenhouse Effect

One constant in our vineyard is the need to replace vines that have died. This loss of vines is commonly referred to as "attrition" and is defined in the dictionary as "a gradual diminution in number or strength due to constant stress".

No matter how faithful we are to monitor the vineyard for pests, disease and water supply, there are always going to be those vines that die in spite of our watchfulness. It is a fact of life in the vineyard business. Ideally, the percentage of loss is small and does not present a major problem. But in the early years of our vineyard, we made a few mistakes that caused us to have a high attrition rate.

Basically, we had too much vineyard and not enough manpower or time and the weeds overtook the vines in most places. Another contributing cause of attrition was our irrigation system. Though powered by a good well and pump it could not overcome the emitters that got clogged, cutting off the critical water to thirsty plants. Vines that have to compete with giant weeds have it bad enough, let alone when trying to do it without adequate water. It meant death for a lot of our baby vines.

Our sixth season found us needing to replace about 1000 vines. This usually meant sending away to a nursery in California for replacement vines at considerable expense. However, during the previous winter we were given a greenhouse which we erected near our house and vineyard. We were delighted viewing the greenhouse as a significant addition to our business enterprise. With the greenhouse we would not only be able to grow our own replacement vines, but we found there were many others in our area desiring a local source for vines. We decided to produce new grapevines to sell to others. (*Think of the savings for us and the additional income we could realize by putting our greenhouse to work!*) God, in His infinite wisdom, had opened up another avenue of supply for us.

Taking cuttings to produce new vines involves several steps. When mature vines are dormant, the vineyard keeper chooses strong, healthy vines that he wishes to reproduce. He then selects strong shoots from which to take his cuttings and cuts twelve-inch sections of these shoots. After that, he buries the entire cutting in the ground for a period of 3 weeks. The cutting must undergo a time in which it rests and stores up energy for growth on its own. This period underground is called the "callusing period" in which hardened tissue develops over the cut end of the cutting. (If they do not have adequate time underground, they may not develop the root structure needed to support the new leaves.)

Next, the cutting is ready to be rooted in a rich, porous, soil mixture and placed in the greenhouse where temperature and humidity can be controlled. This allows us to get optimum growth from each cutting. It is critical that they develop strong roots before they begin growing their leaves. We keep them watered and warm during the late winter and early spring months so that they can develop into healthy vines that can grow outside our controlled environment. This process takes some time. While each cutting has the potential of growing to be a heavy fruit producer, if it does not have adequate roots, it's potential will not be reached.

A properly functioning church is a lot like a greenhouse. We take a brand new believer in Christ and surround him/her with solid biblical teaching, lots of love and acceptance. In this way we help them grow deep roots of their own to support their new found faith and to enable them to weather the inevitable storms that will come. Once they know *what* they believe, and *why*, they are more able to effectively introduce others to the same relationship they have found.

Just as in our greenhouse we cannot *force* a cutting to grow into a healthy plant, so not every profession of faith produces a strong believer. A person can *profess* to know God but not live a life that evidences true love for Him. It is interesting to note that attrition has another meaning when applied to religion. It is this: *"Repentance for sin motivated by fear of punishment rather than by love of God"*. Our motivation for serving God must be to show our love for Him in every aspect of our lives, including the area of duplicating ourselves (thus duplicating Him) in the lives of others.

> Always be prepared to give an answer to everyone who asks you to give the reason for the hope that you have. But do this with gentleness and respect, keeping a clear conscience...
>
> 1 Peter 3:15-16a

In order to replicate ourselves (meaning the *Jesus* in us), we must be assured of *what* we believe and in *Whom* we believe. In other words, we need to grow up in our faith!

> Therefore rid yourselves of all malice and all deceit, hypocrisy, envy, and slander of every kind. Like newborn babies, crave pure spiritual milk, so that by it you may grow up in your salvation, now that you have tasted that the Lord is good.
>
> 1 Peter 2:1-3

To grow in the Lord requires us to feed on His word, personally! We cannot expect to become fruitful believers and therefore reliable witnesses of the grace of God if we have not matured and grown up in our Christian faith. We do this by putting ourselves in an atmosphere where the growing conditions are favorable for growth! Paul admonished believers on the importance of maturity.

In fact, though by this time you ought to be teachers, you need someone to teach you the elementary truths of God's word all over again. You need milk, not solid food! Anyone who lives on milk, being still an infant, is not acquainted with the teaching about righteousness. But solid food is for the mature, who by constant use have trained themselves to distinguish good from evil.

Hebrews 5:11-14

Remember the parable of the sower we looked at earlier? The seed that grew up quickly but had no roots withered quickly when the scorching sun came upon it. (Matthew 13:21) Thus a believer that has not been grounded in God's Word, runs the risk of falling away from Him if they do not have deep roots in Christ. Our spiritual roots give us stability and support to weather the storms of real life just as the grapevines develop deep roots to withstand the winds and storms in their world.

I challenge you to take a penetrating look beneath you...at your own root structure! What do you see? Do you have deep, mature roots that give you stability when the hurricanes threaten to blow you away? When the tornadoes whirl everything about you and menace your carefully ordered life, are you able to stand firm? Not lose faith? This is the true test of your root system. It is your faith.

It is not too late to redirect your priorities and your focus. Now is the time to prepare for those future storms. During *my* life's roughest storms, I found myself sheltered in my heavenly Father's arms. He has taken me through the trials and not left me alone at any time in the midst of them. *I know* He is willing to do the same for you. Ask Him!

Find comfort in Him. Rest in the knowledge that He never changes. He's got it all under control!

> The Lord is near to all who call on him, to all who call on him in truth.
>
> Psalm 145:18

> Come unto me, all you who are weary and burdened, and I will give you rest...and you will find rest for your souls.
>
> Matthew 11:28,29b

# HARVEST!

The culmination of all our efforts throughout the season is, of course, *the harvest*! Everything we do during the year is moving towards this. Every time we spray to protect against disease, eradicate pests, and to kill the weeds, it is always with the harvest in mind. If we do not manage the field properly all year long, we cannot expect to reap a bountiful harvest of grapes. It is not possible to wait until just a few weeks before picking the grapes to begin training the vines and think there will be a good harvest! The process of planting and harvesting has been going on, worldwide, since creation began. And we are told it will continue until God calls His people home.

> As long as the earth endures, seedtime and harvest, cold and heat, summer and winter, day and night will never cease.
>
> Genesis 8:22

Bill and I petitioned the Lord for His blessing on our work, because without Him, we would not have the vineyard at all! And *He* is ultimately the One in control of our harvest, right?

> For the Lord your God will bless you in all your
> harvest and in all the work of your hands, and your joy
> will be complete.

Deuteronomy 16:15b

The parallels are once again obvious. Everything God does during *our* growing season (while we are on this ball of dirt we call Earth) is accomplishing *His* specific goal. What a precious promise it is that **God** will finish His work in us and bring us to that final perfection for which we long.

> ...Being confident of this, that He who began a good
> work in you will carry it on to completion until the
> day of Christ Jesus.

Philippians 1:6

Sometimes it takes drastic pruning in the vineyard to make a vine fruitful and coax it to its full, fruiting potential. In our own lives, our Heavenly Father's hand may seem harsh and unloving at times, yet it is the very opposite! His great love for us causes Him to continue working in us to bring about a specific harvest in our lives.

> No discipline seems pleasant at the time, but
> painful. Later on, however, it produces a harvest of
> righteousness and peace for those who have been
> trained by it.

Hebrews 12:11

The scriptures more than imply that the crop of "*Righteousness*" is a blessing from God and greatly desired.

> Now He who supplies seed to the sower and bread for food will also supply and increase your store of seed and will enlarge the harvest of your righteousness.
>
> 2 Corinthians 9:10

> Peacemakers who sow in peace raise a harvest of righteousness.
>
> James 3:18

There is also another harvest mentioned in the Bible to which all Christians are looking forward. It is the final harvest of souls when we will be called to our eternal home. Read how the apostle John draws a parallel between earthly and eternal fields and getting ready for the harvest.

> Do you not say, 'Four months more and then the harvest'? I tell you, look at the fields! They are ripe for harvest. Even now the reaper draws his wages, even now he harvests the crop for eternal life, so that the sower and the reaper may be glad together.
>
> John 4:35-36

Then another angel came out of the temple and called in a loud voice to him who was sitting on the cloud, "Take your sickle and reap, because the time to reap has come, for the harvest of the earth is ripe." So he who was seated on the cloud swung his sickle over the earth, and the earth was harvested.

Revelation 14:15-16

We often place the emphasis on very different types of fruit: fame, fortune, oneness with the universe, beauty, health, eternal youth, etc. But nothing from this world can be taken with us and *nothing we do can earn us a place in heaven*. It is as simple as that! There is only one way to eternal life...Jesus!

Christ is the end of the law so that there may be righteousness for everyone who believes.

Romans 10:4

...If you confess with your mouth, "Jesus is Lord," and believe in your heart that God raised him from the dead, you will be saved. For it is with your heart that you believe and are justified, and it is with your mouth that you confess and are saved. As the Scripture says, "Anyone who trusts in him will never be put to shame."

Romans 10:9-11

Make sure you will be a part of that final gathering into God's eternal kingdom known as heaven. There is no fruit we, ourselves, can offer to God of which He will approve. Just as a grapevine left on its own will not bear fruit that is acceptable to the vineyard keeper, there is a specific fruit that our Father will look for when we stand before Him on that last day. Do we bear the name of Jesus Christ? Remember...

> Salvation is found in no one else, for there is no other name under heaven given to men by which we must be saved.

> Acts 4:12

## Meditation Fifteen
# Devastation!

Early spring, 2000: This grape-growing season began with all the high hopes a new season typically brings. We completed our initial pruning while the plants were dormant and the vines were ready to begin the process we had grown to know and love over the years. This was our fifth season in the vineyard, and it promised to be the first season when most of our vines would be producing fruit. We could reasonably expect 8-10 tons off of our 12 acres. This was not at all out of the question given the quality of ground, plentiful water and the age and health of the plants. We were, to put it mildly, ready to reap a bountiful harvest!

> The year: 1987 and I was living my life as a wife and mom and walking with the Lord. I was doing all the "right" things. I was working to make my marriage of 13 years successful and was a stay-at-home mom trying to raise my three boys in the "nurture and admonition of the Lord". I had every reason to expect the blessing of the Lord on our family and everything was going well. Not perfect, but we were making it as a Christian family and we were happy. (Or so I *thought*!)

Mid March and our vineyard began to come alive. First we began to see the buds get fat with their promise of new life. Then the shoots began to grow and push outwards and upwards and reach toward the sky. The new shoots were from 6-10" long now and we were watching expectantly for the blossoms to appear.

Then the unthinkable happened; unexpected and ruinous to our field. A late freeze! Not just a light frost, but a freeze! It didn't last very long, probably just the early morning hours. *(Was it long enough to damage all the new growth or just barely burn the ends?)* We watched and prayed fervently for the latter.

To our dismay, within a few days, we saw **all** the new growth showing signs of dying! ***Oh no!*** *How could this be? This was not supposed to happen!* We had such high expectations and hopes!

The plants themselves were not damaged...*that* was a good thing. But would the plants be able to rebound during *this* season? We had always heard that the grapevine puts out a second, and sometimes a third, bloom that could produce fruit. Perhaps there was only minor damage; we'd just have to wait and see. We could still have a good harvest, right? Surely the Lord would not take that away from us. We would not know the extent of the damage for a month, when the blooms began to set.

Waiting! It is not an easy task to wait...let alone to wait patiently! We determined this was a test for us; perhaps

God wanted to see where we had placed our trust. We did much soul searching and crying out to the Lord. We knew that throughout the scriptures we are exhorted to call upon the Lord in our time of trouble and to *wait* for Him. And in that waiting, we are promised His strength.

> ...Call upon me in the day of trouble; I will deliver you, and you will honor me.
>
> Psalm 50:15

> Wait for the Lord; be strong and take heart and wait for the Lord.
>
> Psalm 27:14

> ...But those who hope in the Lord will renew their strength. They will soar on wings like eagles; they will run and not grow weary, they will walk and not be faint.
>
> Isaiah 40:31

> ...My soul finds rest in God alone; my salvation comes from him. He alone is my rock and my salvation; he is my fortress, I will never be shaken.
>
> Psalm 62:1-2

From the beginning of this bewildering turn of events, Bill and I made a promise to each other. Whenever tempted to despair, we would remind each other of this..."the **Lord** has pruned our vineyard this year. *He* is in control."

It was the spring of 1988 and my husband of 13 years had made his plans to leave me. He had paid the deposit on his new apartment and had his new car. Then our five-year-old son, Zachary, became deathly ill with spinal meningitis and lapsed into a coma. He was very near death! The second day of his hospitalization, our apartment was robbed! *(All our important personal items were taken. I felt so violated!)*

After twelve days, we brought a very frail *32 lb.* Zach home from the hospital, **without the ability to hear**! He was deaf!!! Then one week later, my husband moved out! He left me with three kids and across the country from my family! Naturally, I was devastated! This was not *my* plan and it surely couldn't be God's will that I suffer like this! *How could He let this happen to me?* Hadn't I been pleasing to the Him? Hurting and confused, I struggled to hang on to faith and sanity. Only Jesus could carry me through this pain and only He could give me any meaningful comfort.

Come late April and early May, and the vines were re-blooming. We began to see the disturbing truth. There were *very few new blooms* on our white varieties and there can only be grapes if there are blooms. (The white grape varieties comprised two-thirds of our vineyard.) Our red grapes (the other third) looked better, but still had fewer blooms than we had hoped.

To further demoralize us, we were plagued with grasshoppers. This was the third year of infestation and they had gotten progressively worse each year. They were ravenous creatures eating not only the foliage but the wood of the vines also, often eating around a small cordon or shoot and making it fall off! Even worse, they began to eat our precious fruit as it began to ripen. (*And believe you me, we did not have enough to share!*)

Bill sprayed pesticide to try and get rid of the grasshoppers, but it had a short-lived effect on these greedy pests. This caused further discouragement. We clung desperately to our motto "God has pruned our vineyard" and chose to believe that God would work even in these dire circumstances.

> ...The Lord bestows favor and honor; no good thing does he withhold from those whose walk is blameless.
>
> Psalm 84:11

Four years had now passed since my husband left me. My three boys and I had moved into our own house and were rebuilding our lives. I found raising three boys as a single mom quite a challenge, but I loved them dearly and we were going to make it. I had wonderfully supportive parents and friends to encourage me and help whenever I needed it. God was definitely taking care of us!

*Then an even worse tragedy struck!* I answered a knock at my door at 5 a.m. July 29th only to learn that my oldest son, Joshua (15 1/2 years old) had been killed in an auto accident! **Intellectually**, *I know God* *promises in His word that He will never give us more than we can handle, but I felt this was definitely **past my limit.***

However, after so many years of having walked with God through the good and the bad, my roots (*my trust*) ran deep in Him. I knew in my heart that He would *somehow* carry me through this, too. **And He did just that!** I can say that I have known the comfort of the Lord on a much deeper level than ever I did before all these problems in my life. Though it was extremely painful and I would never wish it on any one, I am able to say along with the Psalmist:

> To the faithful you show yourself faithful...
> You, O Lord, keep my lamp burning; my God
> turns my darkness into light...As for God,
> His way is perfect; the word of the Lord is
> flawless. He is a shield for all who take refuge
> in Him. For who is God besides the Lord?
> And who is the Rock except our God? It is
> God who arms me with strength and makes
> my way perfect.
>
> Psalm 18:25-28, 30-32

Harvest time finally arrived, but we had no idea how pitiful it would be. Our two white varieties came in at an alarmingly low *combined* weight of 1060 lbs. (The previous season we had a combined weight of 3500 lbs.) One of our red grape varieties produced a mere 250 lbs. of grapes, while the other (which had yielded 5000 lbs. the previous year), only gave us 1400 lbs. This was more than appalling! Our entire field yielded slightly over one and a half tons! *Inconceivable*!

We desperately looked for something positive (*anything*!) in this depressing situation. The only positive we could think of was this: because the vines had little or no fruit to carry this year, they had been strengthening and deepening their roots. This *should* mean that the next season we would have an even greater harvest than normal. In other words, all the energy they had been storing up this season would be released in a beautiful, bountiful harvest during the next growing season.

Spiritually speaking, we had been learning to trust in the Lord on a deeper level than before. We may never understand the why of this season. But the truth is, God takes even the bad and brings good from it. This is a precious fact that has encouraged me through each and every trial in my life.

> And we know that *in all things* God works for the good of those who love him, who have been called *according to his purpose*.
>
> Romans 8:28, Italics mine.

Less than one year after Josh's death, God did indeed bring something good my way. He brought me a wonderfully fun, fantastic, godly man to ease my loneliness and pain and to be a wonderful dad to my two sons. We met on a blind date and exactly 8 weeks later (TO THE DAY) we were married! I could not have orchestrated this scenario and it was definitely God's timing, not my own. If I had my choice, I would have done this **years** before but I now understand I had a lot of learning and growing to do before I was ready to be married again.

We have now had two decades of love, friendship, laughter, tears and spiritual adventures together. I know we can look forward to the future with confidence in our loving heavenly Father Who will always be by our side, through thick and thin, triumph and tragedy ... And always ready to carry us when we do not have the strength to stand.

Nowhere in the Bible are Christians promised a life of ease while here on earth. We can, however, look forward to the future when the reality of heaven will be revealed to us in all of its peace and tranquility.

> He will wipe every tear from their eyes. There will be no more death or mourning or crying or pain for the old order of things has passed away.
>
> Revelation 21:4

In the meantime, we must learn the invaluable lesson of contentment. Contrary to popular opinion, joy does not find it's source in what we have or do not have.

...For I have learned to be content whatever the circumstances. I know what it is to be in need, and I know what it is to have plenty. I have learned the secret of being content in any and every situation, whether well fed or hungry, whether living in plenty or in want. I can do everything through Him who gives me strength.

Philippians 4:11-13

Whenever you are faced with the seemingly insurmountable trials, meditate on the following verses. This passage will encourage you to place your trust in the Lord, and in Him only. Only then will you find true and abiding peace for your soul. Not *happiness* in your circumstances, but ***real peace in spite of them***!

Rejoice in the Lord always. I will say it again: Rejoice! Let your gentleness be evident to all. The Lord is near. Do not be anxious about anything, but in everything, by prayer and petition, with thanksgiving, present your requests to God. And the peace of God, which transcends all understanding, will guard your hearts and your minds in Christ Jesus.

Philippians 4:4-7

# LETTING GO

*For I know* the *plans I have* for you", declares the Lord, "plans to prosper you and not to harm you, plans to give you hope and a future. Then you will call upon me and come and pray to me, and I will listen to you. You will seek me and find me when you seek me with all your heart.

Jeremiah 29:11-13, italics mine

Another winter had passed and it was now 2001. After the previous year's setback in the vineyard, we cautiously, but optimistically, looked forward to the coming year's season. We had placed our last harvest behind us and realized that we needed to continue to place our trust in the *Lord* of the harvest, not in the harvest itself. Maybe God desired to redirect our steps. As our heavenly Father, He is continually moving us, challenging and fine-tuning our lives to make us fit for heaven. (We do the same with our children, don't we? We train them to be morally responsible, godly adults so they may be a credit to us and to society.)

In our disappointment over the previous season, we reaffirmed that we had actually heard from God *in the beginning* of this enterprise and were not of His will. Since last season had been such a setback, we wanted to make sure God wasn't telling us that we should get out of the business, maybe even that we were wrong to begin the vineyard at all! We re-examined our beginnings and re-checked our motives.

Finding no reason to doubt our initial leading, we determined God was testing our loyalties and our motives *today*, right now! We believed God did not want us to give the vineyard up, but to give it up *to Him*. He wanted us to wait upon Him and *His* timing in the vineyard. Was our heart still His? Were we willing to accept a change in plans and follow Him wherever He led…no matter what? These were very important questions with which we wrestled.

As humans, we often forget that God is a jealous God! He will not allow *anything* in this world to take our affections and loyalties from Him. When something does, He takes steps to draw our attention to the offending attitude or "thing" so we may rectify the situation and get our priorities straight! In the book of Matthew, Jesus pointed out that we'd better be sure our treasure is in the right place.

Do not store up for yourselves treasures on earth,
where moth and rust destroy, and where thieves break
in and steal. But store up for yourselves treasures in
heaven...

For where your treasure is, there your heart will
be also.

Matthew 6:19-21

How often have we heard the question "If God loves
me, why would He let something like this happen to me?"
My response is simply this; that God loves us and has only
our best in mind. When my sons were young and they
asked me for something that I knew would not be good for
them, I felt free to tell them "no". It was because I wanted
the *very best* for them. Did they always agree with my idea
of what was good? Of course not, but I knew better because
I had much more experience in life and I was looking at the
long-term effects.

In the same way, I can trust that God will give me
*anything and everything* **that is good for me**. But I have to
keep in mind that He thinks a lot differently than I do as
He says in Isaiah:

"For my thoughts are not your thoughts, neither are
your ways my ways," declares the Lord.

Isaiah 55:8

As Bill and I began the season with new hope that God was going to "bless the socks off us", we consciously placed the future of the vineyard *in His hands*. He had never let us down in the past and we knew He never would. Either we would have a tremendous crop (which was our *ardent* desire), or He would show us another way. So, we settled in to work, wait and see!

Do *you like to wait?* I sure don't! Waiting is seldom easy. But we are exhorted in the scriptures quite often to do just that...WAIT!

> Wait for the Lord; be strong and take heart and wait for the Lord.
>
> Psalm 27:14

> Those who know your name will trust in you, for you, Lord, have never forsaken those who seek You.
>
> Psalm 9:10

There is tremendous relief in placing our trust in a God Who knows all and sees all...not having to trust only in ourselves with our limited vision and understanding! We could be free from worry about the coming season and **rest**! But it was a *choice to do so!* Though a great deal hung on the vineyard production this year, we knew God had it all under control.

Of course, there were all sorts of niggling doubts that tried to steal our peace. *Would we get another freeze? Would hail get the crop? Would disease wipe out our vines? Would we have the finances to overcome last year's loss?* All these questions were laid at the feet of Jesus more than once and there I found peace. For I know that

> ... (the) Peace of God, which transcends all understanding, will guard your hearts and your minds in Christ Jesus.

> Philippians 4:7

In each of our lives we have situations that either drive us mad or drive us to Jesus. You see, God knows that if we *can* handle a situation on our own, we will most certainly do so! We will have no need to turn to Him for help. But when we are at the end of our rope, we either have to let go and fall on His mercy, or frantically fight to hang on in our own waning strength, not knowing how long before either help arrives or we fall.

So knowing all of this, take a moment to stop and discover what it is that threatens to undo you...personally. Is it financial worry? Marital disharmony? Child related despair? Unforgiveness? Loneliness? Insecurity?

It is vitally important that you make *a conscious* effort to take each situation to Jesus and lay it down, give it up! I find this is not a one-time event, but one that must be repeated constantly. (Remember old habits are hard to break and *it takes time.*) Tell Him that you relinquish control of each situation and accept His will in and through you and your troubling circumstances. **That is where peace is found, nowhere else.** Then pray that He will show you what, if any, steps are to be taken *by you*. Do only those things and then *practice* the fine art of *WAITING* on Him for the outcome. Don't worry, He will not fail you. Drop into His outstretched arms and have assurance that *He will catch you.*

# BLACKROT!

Unbeknownst to us, our season of testing was to continue. We began the season by hiring a couple of laborers to do the winter pruning in the vineyard. *(What a blessing that was not to have to do all the work ourselves!)* With that out of the way, we were able to use our time to complete some much needed repairs to the vineyard posts, wires, watering system, etc. We also planted about 1000 new vines to replace some of those missing. We were more *prepared* for this season to begin than we had ever been before.

As the date of the last year's freeze (April 9th) came and went, we breathed a sigh of relief and felt confident that, at least, we wouldn't have to face *that* situation again. Then on April 17th, we woke with the dreadful memory that the forecast had been for possible freezing temperatures! *(At this late date...could you believe it?!)* Bill checked the thermometer just before sun-up and it was at 34 degrees!

Would it continue to drop before the sun came up and began warming the air? Surely we wouldn't suffer the same fate as last year? Our vines already had 6-15" shoots with blooms. We would lose it all if the temperature dipped any further. While panic knocked at our door, Bill and

I reminded ourselves *and each other* where our trust was. You know it is easy to *say* we have put our trust in God in a given situation, but it is an entirely different matter to have actually done so. (*It has been my experience that there is usually a test to see if we are serious and where our trust **really** is.*) The truth becomes obvious when the test comes and we see whether we remain at peace, or not. While we awaited the outcome, we found that *we actually had peace!* It was amazing not to worry when there was so much at stake!

And let's not forget the *fruit* produced during a test from God! Remember the passage in James about perseverance?

> Blessed is the man who perseveres under trial, because when he has *stood the test*, he will receive the crown of life that God has promised to those who love Him.

> James 1:12, italics mine

Well, back to that near freezing morn…the sun came up, quickly warming the air. The vineyard showed no ill effects. We were elated and praised the Lord. We had passed the test! Surely we were "home free" now, right?

The vines were now covered in fruit-set blooms and we had every indication of a bumper crop! Yes, we still struggled with the inevitable problems associated with farming: like broken equipment, needing chemicals that were stored elsewhere, inclement weather at a time when Bill needed to spray fungicide, and the ever present problem of emitters getting clogged, etc. But in spite of these, this seemed to be a near perfect season.

The weather was exceptional: lots of rain, just when we needed it throughout the late winter, spring and early summer (great for the vines), cool temperatures that accompanied the rains (which lessened the likelihood of Blackrot), mild days (not the usual high temperatures that stressed the vines). It was perfect! And the vines showed their enjoyment by carrying very heavy loads of grapes.

Our ease was short lived. A new test was upon us. **Blackrot!** It was late May and the temperatures were in the upper 80's. The humidity and warmth were perfect for the Blackrot to spread and it was doing just that! We were not overly concerned because Bill was skilled in detecting and controlling this fungus. The solution was relatively simple... spray fungicide. So that is just what he did. But the Blackrot didn't go away like it supposed to. So he sprayed again in 7 days, as the chemical label instructed. Still the Blackrot spread!

This was getting serious. Our fruit was beginning to suffer damage. We were at a loss as to what more we could do. We prayed earnestly for the answer, but seemed to get no response. Bill sprayed the vineyard several times over the course of the next month. (Not only was this time consuming, hot work late at night...but it was *expensive*!) And while we prayed and pleaded for the answer, the heavens still were silent as more and more of our crop was destroyed!

Then one day, through a totally unexpected source, we got our answer. Our field had developed a resistance to the chemicals we were using. Bill had been alternating between two different types (we thought) but discovered they were just variations of the same one. We finally had our explanation! We quickly purchased another type of chemical and applied it and the Blackrot finally stopped! What a relief! *Our* timing for the answer would have been very different, but God worked it out *in His time*. Just one more lesson as we continued to practice our new habit of trusting in God, not in ourselves.

> Trust in the Lord with all your heart and lean not on your own understanding; in all your ways acknowledge him, and he will make your paths straight.
>
> Proverbs 3:5

Am I saying this was easy? No way! Everyone knows how easy it is to form bad habits, but it is so much more difficult to break them and form good ones. We were making a conscious effort to practice a new habit of trust and working hard to break our old habit of worry. I once heard someone say that worry is the least enjoyable sin. When you think about it, it's true! Other sins you can name have at least temporary pleasure, but worry only makes you feel bad, and worse. And what does it accomplish? Nothing! We usually can't change a single thing about the future!

You know…Blackrot has many of the same consequences as sin. If left untreated it will completely destroy any hope of quality fruit. And it is UGLY! When sin is small, it can be eradicated with relative ease. But when we give it full rein, it eats away at our soul and darkens our hearts. Consider these words.

> For although they knew God, they neither glorified him as God nor gave thanks to him, but their thinking became futile and their foolish hearts were darkened.
>
> Romans 1:21

We must be careful not to let harmful habits become entrenched sins that cripple us and cloud our judgment. Sin is so much easier to eliminate in the beginning before it becomes a stronghold. The longer we wait to break the old, sinful habits, the harder it becomes. So, be on your guard! Catch those sins when they first try to take hold and replace them with good habits that benefit you and please the Lord. Take whatever steps are needed to get rid of the disease that plagues you. And remember; it takes practice… and more practice…and more practice still to become holy! And this process will not be complete until we see Jesus and He takes us home.

# Plague

Our seasons of trials seemed interminable. Would they never end? We were beginning to wonder. This next season blew in with several severe storms packing very high winds (*60 mph, northern winds*). A north wind was unusual at this time of year when the vines already had a full complement of leaves. The high winds caused *many, many* vines to blow down, either partially or completely. This caused a lot of additional work to tie them back into place. (*More labor; just what we needed!*) To say nothing of the fact that it was very hard on the vines.

And then...the grasshoppers returned! I don't mean just a few, I mean they *swarmed* all over our vines, our ground, everywhere! The year before, we had been told that after three years the grasshoppers would get a disease and die out. This was now the fourth year! We were definitely unprepared for this! It was dreadful and I hated even being outside because they would hop on me and around me and....yuck!

The "hoppers" arrived in late May and by early July we had suffered quite a bit of damage to both our vines and our grapes. The outer edges of the vineyard were decimated and the critters were eating their way towards the center at an alarming rate! Some vines had only fruit left, no leaves!!! In some places, there were whole clusters under the vines because the grasshoppers were cutting the stems causing them to fall to the ground. This was getting to be more than we thought we could bear.

I cannot adequately convey to you the disappointment that threatened to overwhelm us. We struggled desperately to cling to our trust in God's love for us and *His ultimate plan* for our lives, but why was He allowing this to happen? Were we doing something wrong? Or was there something we were not doing, but should be?

We decided to invest the money to have a crop duster spray a potent pesticide over our entire vineyard (another big expense). He sprayed our vineyard on a Thursday night. The grasshoppers began dropping dead everywhere and we were thrilled, as you can well imagine.

Friday we saw dead hoppers all around. On Saturday afternoon we began to see some live ones again and by Sunday afternoon, the voracious insects once again overwhelmed the perimeter of the vineyard. *All that money and not even three days of relief from them! (Groan!)* How did we deal with this newest frustration? With much difficulty, I can assure you. *(One day, as I was mowing the vineyard and they were hopping all around and on me, I actually screamed in frustration and vowed that was it…I was going to give up and forget even trying. This was short lived, but I was just so tired of facing all these disappointments!)*

Both Bill and I grappled with the hurt and disappointment. Our only hope of surviving, with any measure of sanity, was to remember that this world is not our home. We are heaven bound. This is only a *temporal* situation. God directed me to First Peter where I read…

> Praise be to the God and Father of our Lord Jesus Christ! In his great mercy he has given us new birth into a living hope through the resurrection of Jesus Christ from the dead, and into an inheritance that can never perish, spoil or fade–kept in heaven for you who through faith are shielded by God's power until the coming of the salvation that is ready to be revealed in the last time. In this you greatly rejoice though now for a little while you may have had to suffer grief in all kinds of trials. These have come so that your faith–of greater worth than gold, which perishes even though refined by fire–may be proved genuine and may result in praise, glory and honor when Jesus Christ is revealed.
>
> 1 Peter 1:3-7

Again we encouraged one another by reflecting on how God had carried us through our years together and from the very establishment of the vineyard. He would certainly not leave us now. We resolved to continue to trust and Bill declared: **"I'm just *not* going to worry!"**

Once again, he prepared to spray pesticide, though we knew that its effectiveness would probably last, at most, a week. We would do our best at what we knew to do, then trust and **wait**! (*Ugh! How much waiting can a person stand? Can you tell me? Obviously God knew we could stand more than we had so far.*)

The next couple of months were much more of the same: doing all we knew to do, knowing that God would ultimately bring about whatever results were best for us. Simply one foot in front of the other, trudging through this wilderness, we knew this season would ultimately end and we *would* survive, though we were unsure how. God was our only place of rest, **the only rest**, for our weary minds and hearts.

> Come to me, all you who are weary and burdened, and
> I will give you rest.
>
> Matthew 11:28

I know I am not alone in having felt *that* uncertain and weighed down with hurts and cares? Who hasn't been terribly discouraged? The real question is, were you able to go to the Lord and seek *Him* and *His will* and find rest? We usually try to make it in our own strength first, right? We use all our knowledge and power trying to accomplish what

God is just waiting to have us turn over to Him. Until we relinquish a situation to Him and allow Him to work as He knows best, things will never be as they should be. This is true in *any* relationship, *any* situation and *at any time.*

If you have not yet been able to find that place of rest, there is no time like the present. Bow your heart and knees and ask the Lord for *His* direction. Release the situation *and its outcome* to Him and trust Him to do the *BEST* thing for you. He is waiting for you to come to Him. He truly wants you to cease from worry and striving in your own strength and be able to rest. Listen to Jeremiah:

> Stand at the crossroads and look; ask for the ancient paths, ask where the good way is, and walk in it, and you will find rest for your souls.

> Jeremiah 6:16

We do know there will be more trials but we also know that Jesus will take us through them, as well. We learned this lesson of trusting in God *in all situations* in the vineyard. We don't really like to hear this, but He tells us we *are going to have trouble* in the world, but it's okay. *He's got it handled!*

> I have told you these things, so that in me you may have peace. In this world you will have trouble. But take heart! I have overcome the world.

> John 16:33

*Thank you, Lord, for Your patience with us and for not giving up on us, even in our stubbornness and pride in our own strength. We want to be pleasing to you, even in our trials. Help us look not just at the NOW but look to the future when we will be forever in heaven with you. Then it will have been worth it all.*

# BOUNTEOUS HARVEST!

> Be patient, then, brothers, until the Lord's coming. See
> how the farmer waits for the land to yield its valuable
> crop and how patient he is...You too, be patient and
> stand firm, because the Lord's coming is near.
>
> James 5:7-8

Harvest time was finally upon us and friends, relatives
and acquaintances were ready to help with harvesting our
grapes. Many of them had been following our progress
over the years and always eagerly anticipated sharing in the
unique experience of a grape harvest.

Bill and I had different responsibilities in preparing
for harvest. I was in charge of contacting the prospective
pickers and planning, purchasing and preparing the food
and drinks for everyone. Bill cleaned all of our 5-gallon
picking buckets and checked all the clippers to make sure
they were sharp and in good working order for each worker.
Then he cleaned and put the large picking bins on the
trailer and weighed them before we started.

It was always our goal to make the harvest experience
an enjoyable one for our pickers, in spite of the sweltering
heat that usually accompanied this time of year. To this

end, we placed two pickers on each row, one on either side of the vine. As they worked their way down the row harvesting the grapes, they got the opportunity to renew an acquaintance with an old friend or perhaps make a new one. This helped to pass the time and everyone enjoyed the fellowship. It was great! (*Our harvesters tended to return year after year, enthusiastic to help again.*)

Even the kids held important responsibilities during our harvest. The youngest children carried *empty* buckets to waiting pickers so they could keep working. The older ones retrieved full buckets and emptied them into the large bins waiting on the trailers. (*FYI: Each bucket holds approximately 20 lbs. of grapes, so the kids got a good workout!*)

We always provided plenty of ice cold drinks throughout the harvest and had a shade set up in case someone needed to get out of the sun. (*Don't want anyone to get heat stroke or anything, you know?*) As mid-day neared and the heat became too intense, we invited the harvesters in to our home for a nice lunch (in the air conditioning) as a special "thank-you". Their work was over and we could not have done it without them.

At the beginning of this season, our estimate was approximately 17 tons of grapes. (The grapevines were loaded with fruit and, considering the age and condition of the vines, we figured this to be a fair *guess-timate*.) At the end of the season, after all four varieties were harvested, we got a total of about thirteen tons. This was several tons below our estimate due to the grasshoppers and Blackrot damage, but definitely an improvement over our previous years.

All in all, I must say this had been a very *interesting* season. High hopes in the beginning, dreadful fears in the middle and our dream fulfilled in the end. We had produced beautiful, quality fruit that was in demand by many purchasers. As a matter of fact, we did not have enough to supply all the demand and that is a good place for a grower to be.

God had proved Himself faithful once again and we had made it through yet another season. The lessons we had learned were filed away for the future and would stick with us long after this season had ended. Our faith had been tested and strengthened and we had seen God move in ways far different than we would have chosen. But He had still brought about a good crop. He truly was, *and IS*, the Lord of the harvest!

# MUSTARD SEED

Harvest was over and we had just returned from a much anticipated (*and needed*) vacation. There had been rain in our absence and the weeds in the vineyard had grown considerably. Not only was it unsightly but it made for a great deal of mowing. My mind wandered aimlessly as I sat once again on the noisy slow-moving tractor.

Every once in a while I would notice a large expanse of native Bermuda grass in the midst of the tall, ugly weeds. There were few weeds in these patches of grass and it got me to thinking. (*What else is there to do for hours on a tractor but THINK!*)

Where did this lovely grass come from? We certainly didn't plant it yet it was interspersed throughout the vineyard, far away from the fringes where anyone may have planted it. So how had it gotten here?

With my superior powers of deduction, I surmised that perhaps a bird had dropped some grass seeds while flying over or perhaps stopping in for a snack on our ripe grapes. Then again, the wind could have blown seeds from neighboring yards. Either way, the grass was spreading and overtaking more and more territory in the vineyard.

I have been told that a characteristic of Bermuda grass is that it takes over an area and inhibits other vegetative growth. In this case, the weeds were being choked out wherever these patches of grass were established so there were pleasant areas of short grass amidst the weeds. *(Are you beginning to get where I am headed with this?)*

All of the sudden the somewhat dim light in my brain began to shine. Amazing! What a wonderful picture of how the *seed* of the Word of God *planted* in a sinful world can establish a pleasant, peaceful oasis amidst the chaos and clamor of sin.

When I finally recognized the analogy, God began to develop it further with me. How often have we wondered what one Christian can do in a world that is often antagonistic to anything God has to say? I have been guilty of thinking my input could not possibly make a significant difference in such a vast, indifferent world. But God has reminded me how a small, seemingly insignificant, seed can effect major changes in an environment.

> The kingdom of heaven is like a mustard seed, which a man took and planted in his field. Though it is the smallest of your seeds, yet when it grows, it is the largest of garden plants and becomes a tree, so that the birds of the air come and perch in its branches.
>
> Matthew 13:31-32

Now equate the weed-infested vineyard to a world full of sins that disfigure and devalue our humanity. In comes *the seed* in the form of a word of forgiveness and new life found in Jesus Christ. The seed takes root in the heart of the Hearer and it begins to grow. That person tells another, and then another and the law of multiplication performs its miracle. As the seed of the Word of God grows, sins are forsaken, peace is found and victory is achieved. Now we have a haven (of righteousness) in the middle of the madness.

> Now he who supplies seed to the sower and bread for food will also supply and increase your store of seed and will enlarge the harvest of your righteousness.

> Matthew 9:10

When you consider the humble beginnings of Christianity (Jesus and twelve disciples) you see the principle of seed planting in its finest form. Jesus came in the form of a man, lived a perfect life and died to secure the only way for us to have a personal relationship with the Heavenly Father, the Creator God of the Universe.

> Since we have been justified through faith, we have peace with God through our Lord Jesus Christ, through whom we have gained access by faith into this grace in which we now stand.

> Romans 5:1-2

Christianity has grown to affect the entire world from this small seed. The gospel of Jesus Christ is the *only faith* that does not require a person to fulfill a lot of rules and regulations in order to achieve a place in heaven. It is the *only* faith that gives you an **assurance** that when you become a true believer in Christ and confess Him as your Lord, you are **guaranteed** a place in heaven, bought *not with your perfection*, but with *Jesus'* perfect life, death and resurrection.

> That if you confess with your mouth, "Jesus is Lord" and believe in your heart that God raised him from the dead, you will be saved....for "Everyone who calls on the name of the Lord will be saved."
>
> Romans 10:9,13

So if it does not rely on *your* works and *your* performance, you can't lose it, right? ***WOW!*** When you really get hold of this concept, you realize that you have **peace with God and security in your relationship with Him…PERIOD!!**

> For it is by grace you have been saved, through faith-and this not from yourselves, it is the gift of God-not by works, so that no one can boast.
>
> Ephesians 2:8-9

Let's carry our analogy further as we look at the seed of Christ that has been planted and growing, and its results? Morality becomes the norm, not the exception. Sins (weeds) gradually give way to righteousness and peace. And those who see the effects of a life given over to God are drawn to the Person Who can grant this same peace and tranquility to them. They have found an oasis. And so it spreads.

> Always be prepared to give an answer to everyone who asks you to give the reason for the hope that you have.
>
> 1 Peter 3:15

What happens when a person leaves this oasis and travels into the surrounding world carrying his message of hope? He begins planting seeds of his own and new *oases* are planted, with new sanctuaries spreading throughout the world. More people are impacted with the glorious gospel of forgiveness through Jesus.

NOW...The most important question for you is... **Have you found that place of rest and peace with God?** Have you been forgiven your sins and assured a place in heaven with Him? All that it requires of you is to talk directly to God and **ask Him to forgive you and give you a changed heart**. He is waiting to give purpose and meaning to your life. It doesn't require fancy rhetoric or complicated songs and dances; just sincerity of heart. Then you, too, will be able to partake of:

> ...the peace of God, which transcends all understanding, ...(and) guards your hearts and your minds in Christ Jesus.
>
> Philippians 4:7

# LAST STRAW

Perhaps you are one of the rare persons whose life has actually followed the course you had planned when you were young. Well my life *doesn't even slightly resemble* what I thought it would be. That's not to say it has not had its thrilling moments and rewarding surprises, because there have been those; but in such very different ways than I had anticipated (as I've shared earlier in this book).

I grew up as the oldest of four daughters in a home where my parents remain married *and love each other.* This secure, loving, middle-class family was the basis for my believing that I could accomplish anything to which I set my mind; a very good foundation for life.

However, I now realize I was like a young grapevine that had lived all its life in a greenhouse, sheltered from any wind or sudden temperature change. (Should you transplant that tender vine into the harsh elements out of doors, it would suffer trauma at the extreme temperatures and strong winds. Why? It is because the vine had not developed the strength to *bend* with the wind or withstand any stress.)

In the beginning, my life was predictable and I was content to remain in my "greenhouse" living my sheltered life for the Lord. But God wanted more from me, as He does from you. He wanted me to be able to withstand the ravages of a capricious and often harsh world, not merely be *alive,* but thrive and be content!

Hence my life became a roller coaster of the unpredictable and here I found myself...a FARMER!!! (*Yes, I had finally accepted the fact that growing grapes was farming. Understand that I had vehemently argued that we were not farmers because we could control watering and were not dependent on rain...ha!)* After the hardships of the last several years, Bill and I had prayed for the Lord to make it clear to us whether we were to continue growing grapes or if it was time to move on to something else. Little did we suspect we would have such a definitive, undeniable answer to our query! We still had much to learn as our heavenly Vineyard Keeper took out His shears to do some more pruning. (*UGH! Again?!)*

In our minds, this was to be *the* **redeeming season.** (*You know, the one that paid for itself and made up for all the labor and pain of the past seven seasons?*) We could reasonably expect about 25-30 tons of grapes by season's end, considering the age and maturity of our vines. A good harvest would go a long way to paying off debt we had incurred in the pursuance of our dream.

Financial gain had taken longer than we had anticipated; but this was the year and we were ready.

The cool spring prevented a dreaded early bud-break and in late March, our Chardonnay and Muscat budded out with the Merlot following close behind. Grateful that the chance of freeze was past, we watched as the shoots grew 2"-8" long. Then April 2nd sneaked in with a mild freeze. Yes, I said a *freeze!!* We maintained our calm (*we had learned some things along the way about not panicking*) and inspected the vineyard carefully. We decided (optimistically) that we had not gotten burned *too badly*. Whew! We breathed the proverbial "sigh of relief" thinking this was entirely too close for our comfort!

A week passed and *another 'norther'* blew in with 32 degree temps; then again, only a day later on April 9th, still another frost caught us!! *UNBELIEVABLE!!* Not just one, but three mornings of 31-32 temps after the tender shoots had timidly ventured forth, believing it was safe for them to begin their new growth. As you can guess, our optimism changed rapidly as we watched much of our future wilt, turn brown and **die!** Here we were again, barely treading water in an all too familiar ocean of hopelessness.

But again, God was waiting to throw out His life preserver and save us from drowning in our despair. We grabbed hold of our faith knowing that our Lord loved us and would bring purpose and meaning even in this new challenge…"because God has said, 'Never will I leave you; never will I forsake you.'" (Hebrews 13:5b)

We were grateful for the blessing that the Cabernet had not yet broken bud when the freezes occurred so it was only mildly affected. Eagerly we watched as tentative new growth appeared and the injured vines pushed out new shoots. We prayed for grapes on these shoots. Oh, how we prayed, because surely this was the Lord's will for us!!

The season progressed slowly with its daily doldrums and duties. Bill sprayed the vineyard ten times against fungus (more this season than any previous) to make sure we did not have a repeat of last season's rot. This was tiresome and expensive, but we could not afford to do otherwise.

When we re-assessed our crop after the freeze damage, we thought we might have as much as 17 tons. It was not as much as we had originally estimated, but still an amount we would be able to live with. We prayed and God sent buyers for **all** our anticipated tonnage which caused us to rejoice! But as the season progressed further and the quantity of fruit became more evident, Bill began to have serious doubts that we would have as much crop as we were anticipating.

Bill and I had come to the decision that this was to be our last season in the vineyard, so we hoped to go out with a "**BANG**"! At least we could pay off debt and have great fruit so our *reputation* as good grape growers would be recognized. (*No one wants to leave looking like a failure!*) However, to our Vineyard Keeper this must have resembled a "bull shoot" like those I so diligently prune from our vines. (*Remember? A bull shoot siphons off nourishment from the main cordons where the fruit is growing and grows big and strong without producing any fruit.*) The ambition to have a good reputation catered to our own egos, but would not accomplish what the Lord desired for us: to walk with Him in obedience and contentment and let our reputation be His concern. So we had to face this issue head-on and **give it up, too**!

Paul, when writing to the Hebrews, reminds us to keep our '*reputation*' in proper perspective. It is better, by far, to be pleasing to God rather than to cater to human standards.

> So we say with confidence, "The Lord is my helper; I will not be afraid. What can man do to me?"
>
> Hebrews 13:6

It was one week before our first harvest was scheduled and it rained. *The problem?* Chemicals cannot be sprayed on the grapes within 14 days of a harvest. So guess what? Bunch Rot (another disease caused by too much rain!) set in on the Muscat and the Chardonnay. (*The white varieties are more susceptible to everything because their skins are thinner.*) By the time we harvested, the laborers had to spend an inordinate amount of time picking out the rot. This doubled our harvesting costs and correspondingly our quantity of usable grapes fell. Total combined crop on these two varieties was ***a mere 3 tons!!!*** Demoralizing!!

Though we were more confident of the Merlot crop (*the previous season we had harvest 8 tons on this one variety*) when harvest came, we got about 3.25 tons. There were a lot of clusters of grapes, but they were extremely small with only 5-8 grapes per cluster. Now reality began to crush us hard! But God was not yet done, for we had still not come to the end of ourselves. (*Just about, but not quite.*) We still had a good crop of Cabernet to rescue some semblance of our dignity (*we thought*).

TIMELINE: Two weeks before our last and final harvest the contracted buyer of all our Cabernet decided he would not honor his contract with us and he backed out! *REALLY!?* Okay, now we had received **THE FINAL STRAW!** We were left scrambling to try and sell our grapes at the end of the season when all buyers have already purchased what they wanted or needed. We were only able to sell about 1 ton and ended up leaving 2-3 tons *hanging on the vines*!

You might well imagine we were completely disheartened after this gut-wrenching season, though we had certainly wrestled with such trials before and survived. Actually, in God's providence and foresight, He had sent our way a teaching series that had really convicted us on the matter of giving up our rights and expectations. We had both individually, and together, finally given the vineyard and our reputation to the Lord. So when we were dealt the final blow, we were able to be at peace. It was astounding! We both experienced that "peace that passes understanding" because we had placed our future entirely into our Father's hands.

In summary, I know that many of the events recorded herein seem unfair and the lessons harsh when looking at them on the surface. However, it is imperative that we realize why God takes such pains with His children, allowing hurt, confusion and distress in our lives. It is because we are to be different and strive towards a loftier goal than non-believers. God will not let His "kids" just drift along with the crowd. Even as I prune my vines (often quite drastically) because I know this will make them even more fruitful, God lovingly prunes and shapes us to make us more into the image of His Son, our Savior.

I diligently disciplined my sons when they were young in order to make them understand and respect authority and so they would be enjoyable to live with. They brought joy to my heart when they obeyed or exhibited qualities I had tried to instill. They "did me proud" on most occasions. But there were other times when they had to be corrected because of the unacceptable behavior so they would understand what my standard was and what was not going to be tolerated. ***What they did reflected on me!***

Did I punish them because I hated them? Of course not! I loved them so much that I forced myself to do what I did not want to do…to cause them pain that would bring repentance. Why? So they would learn. Likewise our

Heavenly Father loves us, only without any misdirected or undeserved discipline. He knows us perfectly and sees into our hearts, so *His* chastisement is exactly suited to our individual needs and situations.

Who of us has not experienced a similar kind of discipline or training? Even though it was painful, are you able to look back and see some spiritual and or emotional growth that took place because of it? We will never reach a place in our lives where we do not need to learn any other lessons and cannot grow any more. And if God is not training us, the most important question to ask is "***WHY***"? If we are His, He *will take the time to make us better.* Consider these words written for all of us:

> And you have forgotten that word of encouragement that addresses you as sons; "My son, do not make light of the Lord's discipline, and do not lose heart when he rebukes you, because the Lord disciplines those he loves, and he punishes everyone he accepts as a son".
>
> Hebrews 12:5-6

Remember: **what we do and who we are, reflects on God.** *Selah! (Think on these things.)*

# EPILOGUE

## THE END...
## AND NEW BEGINNING?

And now we come to the end of our seasons in the vineyard for the last and final time. Has it been worth all the labor, financial hardship and disappointment? Now that some time has passed, we would have to say YES! Granted, if we had known from the beginning what we were in for, we would have opted out and that *right quickly*! (*We are not gluttons for punishment.*) Yet we have seen God move on our behalf and carry us through very difficult times. We have felt His love and concern and known His comfort when nothing else could comfort us. Our roots have grown deeper and our confidence in Him even surer through each trial. And we know that in the difficult times ahead (*for they will most assuredly* come) He will be right there with us.

Our *heavenly* Vineyard Keeper will continue working in *our* lives to improve *and increase* our fruit. I find this a very comforting promise in Philippians, that God will never give up on me until I am completed (*or perfected*):

...Being confident of this, that he who began a good work in you will carry it on to completion until the day of Christ Jesus.

Philippians 1:6

*(Can you imagine? Someday we will be perfect! Wow!)* My day-to-day labor in the vineyard has given me a new appreciation for the love, care, diligence, patience, precision and dedication of our Lord as He works in and through our lives. He has so much He wants to do in us! We must willingly submit to His tender pruning so He will be able to present us as mature, fruitful children to His Father on that final day of harvest.

I don't know about you, but I long to have my heavenly Father be pleased with me when I finally see Him face to face. I want Jesus to be able to say to me the words the Master spoke to *His* servant in the parable of the talents:

> Well done, good and faithful servant! You have been faithful with a few things; I will put you in charge of many things. Come and share your master's happiness.

Matthew 25:21

We are looking forward with excitement to the next phase of our lives. We built a beautiful vineyard full of growing grapevines: some young and not yet productive and some mature and in their prime. We can be proud because we have done our very best and God has multiplied our efforts. Though we may not have succeeded by the world's standards, we believe God is pleased with us. And...**Isn't that what counts?** Because it is, after all is said and done... for the

## VINEYARD KEEPER'S GLORY!